L.L. Bean
Saltwater
Fly-Fishing
Handbook

L.L. Bean
Saltwater Fly-Fishing Handbook

LEFTY KREH

Illustrations by

BILL BISHOP JR.

The Lyons Press

Printed in the United States of America

10 9 8 7 6 5 4 3 2 1

Library of Congress Cataloging-in-Publication Data is available on file.

CONTENTS

III. FISH

Introduction

The fastest-growing segment of the fascinating sport of fly fishing is salt water. Many who are heading to the shore are newcomers, but most are freshwater fly fishermen. There are a number of reasons why a freshwater fly fisherman would want to pursue saltwater fish: There are many species; the fish are often larger and stronger; and in many areas, you can fish year-round. People often travel to escape the winter cold to cast to fish in warmer waters. In short, salt-water fly fishing will broaden your horizons.

There are fundamental procedures for all saltwater fly fishing. But one of the fascinations of this sport is that it requires mastering different techniques for differ-ent species. You don't fish for snook the same way you would for striped bass. Albacore require a different technique than do bonefish.

Most freshwater fly fishermen will have to hone their skills. The conventional nine o'clock to one o'clock style of fly casting that works well on a trout stream often doesn't work as well in salt water. Many saltwater fly-fishing guides report that their clients simply can't cast well enough to take advantage of the many opportunities that their guides present. You can't creep to within a few feet of most fish while salt-water fly fishing. Instead, you have to cast heavier flies longer distances. And God doesn't let you cast downwind very often in the salt. But don't let this intimidate you. Instead, it is an opportunity to become a better caster. You don't have to know how to cast 100 feet—but it helps. Fortunately, you don't need a lot of muscle to cast

Snook

Striped Bass

Albacore

Bonefish

You can use a canoe to reach hard-to-find saltwater fishing opportunities.

well. There are many women who are able to throw all the line needed to catch salt-water species.

And you are not limited to where and how you enjoy fly fishing in salt water. You can fish from the shore, wade, or use a canoe or a kayak. You can cast from a johnboat or a bonefish skiff, or fly fish from an offshore cruiser. Some fish can be caught in inches of water, whereas others are caught in the deep sea.

Fly fishing in salt water is the most fascinating, challenging, and satisfying way to catch fish with a fly rod. The information in this book can help you enjoy this sport.

I. BASICS

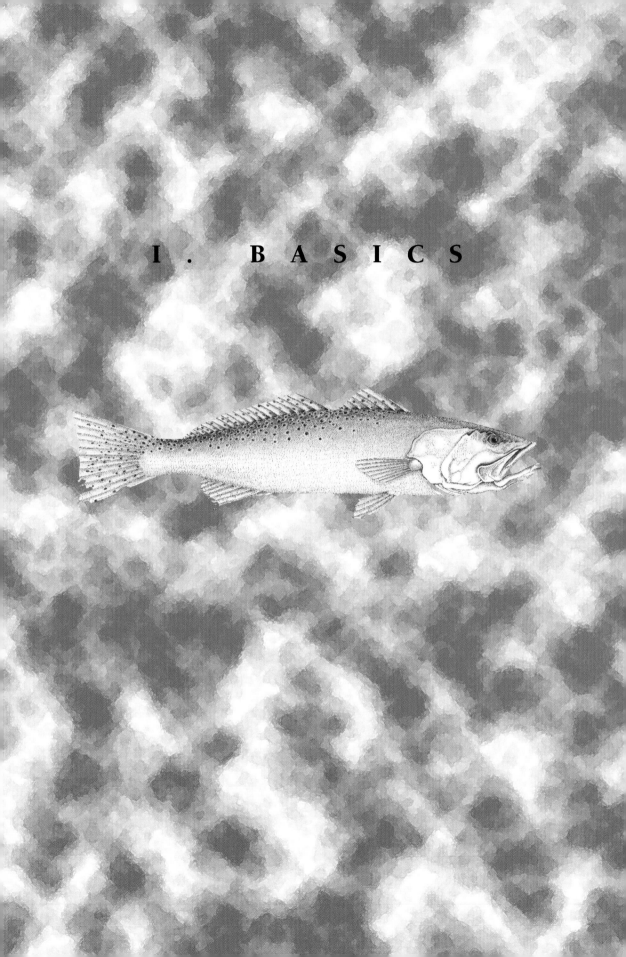

Where

You will need to use different techniques—and sometimes different tackle—to fish the various types of salt water. The types of waters you might fish include the following distinct areas: inshore waters, beaches, flats, backcountry, and offshore. Each of these areas tends to have different types of structure. This affects the way baitfish behave, and in turn, the way the gamefish behave. The following is a brief description of each area.

Inshore

Waters that are within several miles of the shoreline and connect to the sea are termed *inshore*. An example would be an inland bay that connects to the sea. The bottoms of inshore waters may vary greatly and may include deep open areas, channels, reefs, large and small rocks, man-made jetties, underwater wrecks, drop-offs, and a variety of currents. Understanding how each of these can affect your fishing success is vital.

For the fly fisherman, the confirmation of the bottom is one of the most important factors. Anyplace where the bottom descends sharply into deeper water (often this drop-off may be only a few feet in depth), you have a potentially better fishing spot. Tidal currents passing over a drop-off form a vertical eddy. Baitfish are carried

Underwater bars appear as dark areas in the water. Baitfish will congregate there, as will gamefish.

by the current and trapped for a time in this vertical wheel, becoming prey to game-fish lurking behind the drop-off. Waters that sweep toward the wall of the drop-off push the baitfish against the wall and momentarily trap them there. Currents that run parallel to a drop-off will often sweep bait against the side of the drop-off. These are all excellent ambush spots for gamefish and excellent places for fishermen.

Uprising rocks, whether they are coral reefs or large boulders, form eddies on the down-current side of this structure. Predator fish can lay in wait in such quiet waters to ambush baitfish being carried past by the tide.

Any wreck of large structure lying on an inshore bottom is a magnet for the smaller species that seek shelter there. That attracts predator gamefish. Usually chumming will lure the predator within casting distance. I'll explain more about this tactic later.

Beaches

Beaches can be made of sand, or they can be a rocky barrier between the sea and dry land. Montauk Point on the tip of Long Island is a rocky wall. Conversely, the Outer Banks of North Carolina are sand beaches. Sandy beaches form when

Beach areas can be sandy.

Beaches can also be rocky.

the ocean can sweep directly against the shore and pile up sand over the years. Most tropical areas have few beaches. In southern Florida, the Bahamas, and the Caribbean, the shorelines often have coral flats that extend miles, so little sand is deposited to form beaches.

The first thing to understand about any beach is that the tide doesn't usually run toward the beach. Rather, it runs *along* the beach. Imagine the beach is one side of a giant river—the sea. From observation, you know that a river bottom is not perfectly smooth. The sea floor also varies in depth. Watch the waves carefully as they roll toward the beach: If the bottom were perfectly smooth, the waves would hold the same shape until they crash on the sand. But there are bars, holes, even channels in the bottom that affect the flow of the incoming waves.

You can predict where the predators and the bait will be by studying the waves. If, for example, a smooth, incoming wave suddenly breaks apart, you know that an uprising in the bottom has created the rupture. That could mean a drop-off on your side of the rupture, and it may be holding baitfish or the quarry you seek. Channels that flow from an outside bar into the beach are highways for bait and predators and need to be investigated.

This structure temporarily traps baitfish when the waves crash against the rocks. Gamefish wait for the stunned baitfish to be funneled to them.

A boulder-wall beach can be a hot spot, too. The rocks trap baitfish in eddies formed as the waves crash against the rocks. This can be some of the most productive and exciting fly fishing you can experience.

Flats

Many anglers think that flats exist only in the tropical waters, but they exist in all seas. Flats can be defined as those areas that are either dry or nearly so when there are extra-low tides and that are rarely more than a few feet deep at high tide. Many areas of New England have sandy flats where bluefish, stripers, and other species are often found during the warmer months. Of course, the most recognized flats are those in Florida and tropical areas, where permit, bonefish, snapper, tarpon, and other species have been sought by fly rodders for years.

Bonefish like to hide out on flats where the color of the sea floor varies.

Backcountry

This is a unique area that holds a special charm for many fly fishermen. The Everglades in Florida is a good example, but there are backcountry fly-fishing waters all over the world. The backcountry is usually described as subtropical or tropical waters that are neither salt nor fresh, but a mixture of both. They hold many species, such as snook, tarpon, redfish (channel bass), and sharks, and are very, very productive for fishermen. In other areas of the world, barramundi, threadfin salmon, snubnosed dart, and many other exciting, hard-fighting species can be found in backcountry waters.

Baitfish hide in the roots of mangroves until the tide flushes them out to snook and other fish.

Offshore

Offshore fishing is usually conducted out of sight of the land. Very few fly fishermen fish offshore. When they do, the captain usually decides where and how they will fish. The mate rigs teasers, chums, and takes care of all the other factors that contribute to the fishing. In many cases, the offshore crew would rather you use their tackle instead of yours, since they are expert at rigging it. The activity of the fly fisherman offshore is usually just casting to the quarry once the captain has found it and the mate has properly conditioned the fish for a cast. This is not meant to demean offshore fly fishing, but little of the expertise falls on the angler. For these reasons this book will only mention offshore fishing in passing.

CHAPTER 2

Time, Tide, and Temperature

F reshwater fly fishermen learn that certain conditions determine how and when they should fish. Two factors affect fly-fishing success in salt water more than any other: tide and temperature.

Tide

Scientists believe that more than fifty natural conditions affect the tide. The most important factor is the gravitational effect of the moon and sun on the earth. The moon circles the earth every 28 days. If you think of this as a 4-week cycle, you will be able to understand how the tide works.

When the moon and the sun are at right angles to the earth, their gravitational pulls are in slightly different directions, so one tends to cancel out the other's gravitational pull on earth's waters. But when they are fairly well lined up with the earth, the pull of gravity on the earth's waters is much greater.

To understand why the tide rises very high and drops very low—or why it doesn't seem to rise or fall much—examine the 4-week cycle. During the first week, the moon and sun may be at right angles to the earth, so the tide will neither rise very much nor fall greatly. The next week, the moon and sun are somewhat in line, the gravitational pull is much greater, and the tide comes up and then drops down drastically. The third week, the moon and sun are again at right angles, so little rise and fall in tide occurs. During the fourth week, the sun and moon are again exerting a stronger pull on the earth's waters, so there is an extra-high and -low tide. Because the moon rotates around the earth, gravitational pull varies from day to day.

The week that the tide rises higher and falls lower is called a *spring tide,* because the water "springs" up during this week. The next week, the tide doesn't rise or fall as dramatically, and is called a *neap tide*. It's commonly referred to as a *nip tide*.

How can a fly fisherman use this knowledge in a simplified way? Every 2 weeks, the tide repeats itself, and the high and low tide are roughly 1 hour later each day. Let's apply this to a fishing trip. Suppose on a Saturday you had an extra-high in-coming tide at Blue Bell Buoy at 10:30 A.M. and the fishing was fantastic. If you came back the following Saturday at the same time, you may find the conditions the exact opposite. But, if you came back at 10:30 A.M. 14 days from the day you had such good luck, conditions would be about the same, unless there is a major weather change.

Here is another example: You found striped bass feeding well at the mouth of a river yesterday at about noon. If you came back to the same spot the next day at noon, fishing might not be as good. Remember, the tide is roughly an hour later each day. If you hang around, at 1:00 P.M. the conditions will probably be about the same. Nothing in fly fishing is assured, but as far as the tide is concerned, you can figure that a tide cycle will repeat itself every 2 weeks and be an hour later each day.

Most newspapers near salt water will carry the tide tables. But how can you tell whether there is a spring or neap tide? Look at the moon. If there is a quarter moon, a neap tide is occurring. If there is a full or no moon, then a spring tide is in force.

Why is the tide so important? There are several reasons. The most important is the effect on baitfish, such as small minnows, crabs, shrimp, or clam worms—anything that predatory gamefish feast upon. Baitfish do not have a home. This is very important in understanding why the predators we seek are at any given place at a certain time. In a trout stream, there are pools in which sculpins, crayfish, nymphs, and minnows live. This is their home pool, and they will make every effort to stay there. When heavy rains flood the pool, these creatures seek shelter under rocks, cut banks, or behind structure to prevent being swept out of their home pool.

But in salt water, crabs, baitfish, and other foods that predators feed on never fight the tide to stay where they are. They don't have a home, so they allow the tide to carry them hither and yon. For example, alewives, mullet, bunker, or crabs may be located near a certain structure today, and tomorrow the tide may have carried them miles away, requiring you to change your fishing location.

So the fly fisherman must look for places where tides concentrate baitfish. Predator fish congregate in ambush places, where the tide concentrates baitfish, but also where the predator can wait in relatively slow water. Predators do this to get as much food as possible while expending as little energy as possible. If a small bay fills with water during an incoming tide, predator species will be lying just inside the mouth of the bay (the mouth of a natural funnel) waiting for the bait to be swept in. They won't be in the main current, but just off the flowing current, so they can dart out and grab whatever shows up. On an outgoing tide, they will take up their position on the outside of the bay to wait for the baitfish concentration to be carried outward on the falling tide.

Another example of baitfish concentration would be in the backcountry. As the tide rises, bait will move in among the flooded mangroves to feed. This disperses the bait and offers a safe haven among the tree roots, so it would be unproductive to fish there on a rising tide. A falling tide is another matter. During the upper half of a falling tide, fishing would still be minimal because the bait can still hide and feed in the shelter. But during the latter half of a falling tide, the bait must come to deeper water and concentrate in great numbers—a perfect feeding opportunity for gamefish.

Let me give one more example: Many gamefish hang around buoys and channel markers, where they catch crabs clinging to the markers or grab baitfish that lie in the calm current behind the structure. But it usually isn't productive to fish there during strong tidal flows. The predators lying deep below the buoy or marker are not going to burn energy to fight the current. Instead, they lie on the bottom, waiting

Ned Brown caught this snook just off a marker during a slack tide.

An area at low tide.

until the tide slackens (either high or low). Then they move up to where the fly fisherman can get a shot at them.

Learning Structure

The tide also can be a great benefit when you want to learn about the structure in a given area. The worst time to learn a new area is during a high tide, when water covers most structure. Instead, inspect the area at low tide. The bottom is often completely exposed—at least you can see much of it. You will see where ditches run below the surface at higher tides, and you can locate important structure that tells you where baitfish may be trapped during strong tidal flow or where predators might hide. The best time to check out the bottom is when there is a low spring tide, when even more water is removed from the area. It's not a bad idea to photograph some of this structure. Of course, be sure to record something in the photo that will be above the high tide as a reference mark. If you have a GPS (global positioning system), you can use it to mark hot spots for a later time.

The same area at high tide.

The tide has other important effects. Storms can dirty the waters. They would remain dirty for long periods of time if there were no tidal current. But during spring tide weeks, the extra flow of water will flush the area clean and improve fishing.

Temperature

Temperature is just as important to saltwater fly fishing as the tide. Many anglers don't think about temperature as much as they should. It is often critical to success. For example, you will find virtually no striped bass in New England from December to March. The one exception is where warm waters are emitted from power plants and the temperature is artificially elevated. The tide affects the movement of baitfish, and so does temperature. Striped bass abandon New England's waters in the fall, because the cooling waters force the baitfish to move south to warmer waters. The predatory stripers, bluefish, bonito, and other gamefish must follow the bait if they want to eat.

This is as true in New England as it is in Florida or the Bahamas. Bonefish will flee flats as water temperatures drop into the high 60s F. They feed most actively when temperatures range between 73 and 80 degrees. If the water gets much hotter, most bones will often stay off the flats. Bluefish show up along the northern Atlantic when the temperature is just about 70 degrees. The important point is to learn the temperatures at which certain species appear or disappear in your area. The bait will appear just before the bigger fish do. Knowledge of when the bait arrives will let you be ready when your quarry appears. The opposite is also true. When the bait abandon an area, the predators follow.

Temperature is important when fishing for bonefish. If you plan to fish in Bahamas for bones, consider the time of year and what temperature will do. If you fish flats that are a long distance from deep water in midsummer, or from December through March, you may have a problem. In summer these shallow waters will heat up from the exposure to the sun. In the winter a cold front may drop the temperature so low that the bonefish leave. But, if this same type of flat is located close to deep water, your problems may vanish. Each incoming tide brings water from the depths (unaffected by the sun or cold) that flush the unwanted waters from the flats so the bones can feed there.

As baitfish move north along the coast in the spring, they will seek temperatures that they prefer. Early in the season, baitfish will more likely be in shallow bays that have a dark bottom, where the sun will elevate the temperature (often by several degrees) during the day. In the warmer areas, such as the Gulf of Mexico and Florida, cold spells will frequently chase redfish, trout, snook, tarpon, bonefish, and other species off the flats. Once the cold spell has passed, flats that have a dark bottom will often have fish feeding 2 or 3 days sooner than on light-colored flats.

CHAPTER 3

Tackle

Most fly fisherman just can't buy enough gear. Here is a lesson in successful fishing: Whether it is fresh or salt water, the truly experienced and successful fly fishermen usually have a very few rods, a small selection of fly lines, and a minimum of flies. I often compare fly fishermen with those who are really into photography. Many photographers believe that if they buy the newest cameras and equipment, they'll take better pictures. But cameras are like guns: They shoot better than the people who own them. Time spent mastering the basics of good picture taking is better used than the time it takes to select and maintain gadgets. The same philosophy applies to all areas of fishing, whether it is trolling offshore for giant tuna, seeking brook trout in a beaver pond, or hunting for snook in a mangrove.

You need very few rods, lines, and flies. The best advice is to select the equipment that will be effective in your area for the type of fishing you do. Obviously, the equipment you use for giant tarpon would be wrong for school stripers. However, even if you travel widely and fish in many areas for a variety of species, you will still need only a small number of rods, reels, lines, and flies. The following is a review of the essential tackle to enjoy fly fishing in the salt.

Rods

Fly fishing in salt water places special demands on the angler that are not encountered when fly fishing for trout, bass, and other freshwater species. You will find three great problems: You will encounter more wind, you will have to throw a much longer line, and you will be casting heavier and more wind-resistant flies.

If you were only to own one fly rod for fly fishing in salt water, it would probably be a 9-weight. However, it would be a little light for some conditions, and a little heavy for others. The 9-weight is not too heavy for most newcomers, it will throw reasonably large flies to striped bass, handle most tarpon to about 60 pounds, and is an ideal rod for most inshore species. A rod that is 8½ or 9 feet in length is best. Longer rods are tiring to cast and are not really necessary. They are also not as efficient as fish-fighting tools.

A better compromise in rod selection might be to have an 8-weight and a 10-weight rod. The 8-weight would be ideal for many flats species and would allow a delicate presentation of smaller flies in calm conditions. The 10-weight would allow you to throw large bulky flies and heavy sinking lines, and there are few inshore fish that cannot be landed successfully on a 10-weight.

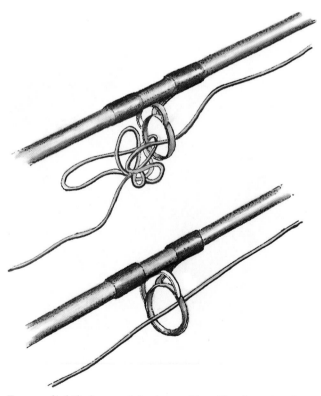

The hardware on a saltwater fly rod is important. Naturally, the reel seat should be strong, and all components on the rod should resist corrosion from the salt. The most important components on a rod are the guides. I don't favor single-foot guides. If you accidentally bend the guide foot, you can bend it back. But the next time you bend the foot and attempt to return it to normal position, it usually breaks. High-grade, chrome-plated snake guides are the best choice. All snake guides and the tip-top should be as large as possible, but not too large to harm the action of the rod. It is better to have large guides, because someday you will have a knot in the fly line as a fish attempts to escape. Small guides cause lost fish.

Even a slightly larger stripping guide will reduce tangles.

The most important guide on the fly rod is the largest one closest to the reel. This is called a butt guide or stripping guide. It acts much like a spinning rod's largest guide. On the cast, fly line does not approach the butt guide smoothly and slither through. Instead, waves and coils flutter toward the butt guide, and if it is small, tangles occur. Some good casters have actually had the line wrap around the butt guide, which killed the cast. For rods size 8 or larger, I recommend a 20-mm-diameter butt guide. Many manufacturers will not put such a large guide on their rods, because cosmetics help sell tackle. An inexperienced fly fisherman who looks at a rod with such a large butt guide may think it resembles a spinning rod, and they will select one that looks more streamlined, with a smaller butt guide. However, if you own a rod that has a stripping guide smaller than 20 mm, most tackle shops have someone who can replace it.

A cigar-shaped handle is popular on small rods used for various panfish and trout fishing. But the cigar-shaped handle has a tendency to move away from the thumb when you stop the rod on the forward cast. The half-wells is a much more efficient handle. In the half-wells style, the upper portion of the handle swells outward. The thumb rests in this swelling and allows you to apply more speed to the cast.

The 8-, 9-, and 10-weight rods will handle almost all saltwater fly-fishing situations, with two exceptions. The first exception is giant tarpon. These fish are found in Florida and a few other places in the world. They range in weight from 90 to nearly 200 pounds. Often, you are forced to fight these fish from an anchored boat. The second exception is for offshore fishing.

For giant tarpon and offshore fishing, a rod's casting performance is not nearly as important as its fighting characteristics. These are often big fish, and the lifting power of the rod is paramount. If you get a giant tarpon close to you and beneath the boat, the only way you can land the giant is to physically lift it to the surface. Once

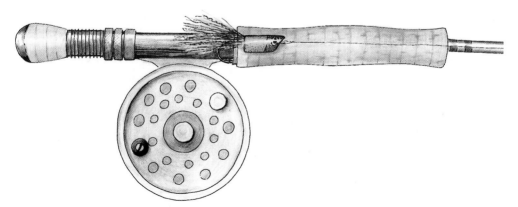

The full- or half-wells grip will help you cast longer distances with greater accuracy and reduce fatigue.

hooked, offshore species seek the depths and try to stay there. If the rod lacks the power to lift these fish, you will never land them.

Fortunately, if you plan a tarpon trip, you will most likely book an experienced guide who has the correct tackle. Many guides prefer that you use their gear, because they know it will be properly rigged. That means you don't have to buy an expensive 12- to 15-weight rod. Some offshore guides carry similar gear.

One fly rod that fly fishermen who fish from the beach or shore might consider is a two-handed rod that has been used in Europe for centuries. However, you don't want to use a two-handed rod that is designed for European fishing, where a great deal of roll casting is called for. Instead, you want to use what is referred to as an overhead-casting two-handed rod. These are at least 12 feet in length, and 14-foot rods are preferred. Several United States rod manufacturers now offer two-handed overhead-casting–style rods that handle lines from size 9 through 12.

Why would you want such a long rod? The longer the rod moves through the casting motion, the more it aids the angler. Longer rods move through a much longer arc and will permit you to make much longer casts than a conventional 9-foot rod. If you have ever cast from shore, you know the wind usually blows in your face, which makes casting more difficult. And so many fish are just beyond the reach of your cast with a normal rod. You can increase the distance of your cast by yards with a two-handed rod.

There is another asset to fishing from shore with a two-handed rod. With a 9-foot rod, the waves often catch the line dropping from the tip and interfere with your retrieve. Also, waves can make lifting line from the water for a backcast troublesome. But with a longer two-handed rod, you can hold the line well above the waves during the retrieve or the backcast. While these are referred to as overhead-casting rods, they do a commendable job when a roll cast is called for.

A final note about two-handed overhead-casting rods: They are not usually recommended in boats. Their proper place is the beach or shore.

Lines

Scientific Anglers and Cortland manufacture more than 400 different fly lines. If you are new to fly fishing, how in the world do you know what to select? Fortunately, you will need only four fly lines for most of your fishing. Although these four won't be perfect for some special fishing situations, they will still do a commendable job.

Let's examine each of these fly lines and why and how we would use them.

Weight Forward

The weight-forward taper is the workhorse of the saltwater fly fisherman. It has a thin, long, level section in the rear, with a gentle taper that swells to a larger level portion (back taper); a thicker portion, called the belly; then another taper toward the thinner front end (front taper). The length of the belly usually determines what the weight-forward line will be used for. If long casts are needed, the belly section should be long. The total length of the front taper, the belly, and the back taper (not counting the rear level line) would be approximately 50 feet or longer. This length allows the line to turn over better when distance is required. The package the line comes in usually has a drawing that illustrates the dimensions of weight-forward line.

Most weight-forward taper lines are not designed for long distance. For the beginner or average saltwater fly rodder, a weight-forward line with a front taper, belly, and back taper should not exceed 42 feet. This type of weight-forward line is usually referred to as a saltwater taper, bug taper, bonefish taper, or tarpon taper. Such lines allow anglers to stand on the bow of a boat with a small amount of line outside the guides, ready to cast. The short heavy belly aids in getting the line quickly to the fish. For the angler who is not a good fly caster, this belly aids in loading the rod, so he or she can obtain a relatively long cast.

Unless you are fishing in deep water, your first choice should be a weight-forward line that floats. Floating line works pretty well to water depths of about 10 feet and will allow you to fish Popping Bugs and streamers. If you want to fish the fly deeper, use a longer leader and allow more time for the fly to sink before beginning your retrieve.

When you need to get the fly down more than 10 feet or search when the tide is running fast (which tends to loft your floating fly line), then a sinking line is needed. In most situations, a sinking *tip* line (the sinking portion will be the first 5 to 10 feet) really doesn't do a good job. Because the front portion sinks, but the rest of the fly line floats, each time you recover line on the retrieve, the floating portion tends to draw the sinking tip upward.

A *full* sinking line is okay, but the rear portion is heavy and often doesn't shoot well through the guides. A better performing sinking line is one in which the first 25 to 30 feet sinks quickly, but is attached to a thin floating line. When it is retrieved, the longer section tends to maintain its depth so that your fly is down where you want it.

This line also has two attributes that endear themselves to fly fishermen. Because the weighted belly is so thin and heavy, it offers very little wind resistance, can be cast more easily into the wind, and is superb for throwing very heavy wind-resistant flies.

Shooting Head

The second line that many people consider essential in salt water is the shooting head, which manufacturers call a shooting taper. This line has an extra-thin rear line, called the running line or shooting line, which is connected to a much larger forward section. The shooting line can be monofilament (usually 30-pound test is

You can make your own fast-sinking lead-core shooting heads. You need a 100-foot or 500-foot spool of Cortland LC-13 Lead Core Trolling Line, some braided mono running line in the 50-pound size (the 30-pound size is too small), and a 100-foot spool of shooting line at least .030″ in diameter. The 50-pound mono running line is a hollow braid. It can be used to connect the shooting line permanently to the shooting head, or you can make a loop at the end and a loop in the shooting line, so you can change heads, if you want.

best), braided line, or a commercial shooting line, which is perhaps the best all-round choice. For salt water, a shooting line should be at least .030″ in diameter. Lines smaller than this may test less than 20 pounds. The forward section of the line—the shooting head—can be a floater, slow or fast sinker, or even a section of lead-core trolling line.

These lines do two things well. When distance is a requirement, no line will do the job like a shooting head, and because the shooting line is so thin—especially when using monofilament—the fast-sinking head can drive your fly deeper into the water.

Other Lines

The level line is one that is simply the same diameter throughout its length and has a limited but important place in saltwater fly fishing. The double taper has a long midsection that is a level line that then tapers at each end. The double-taper line has little use in saltwater fly fishing and can be ignored.

It is important to understand that today manufacturers are making many kinds of lines. You might want to investigate if there is a special line that will work especially well for you. However, the weight-forward and shooting tapers described above will do the job most of the time in most situations in salt water.

A word of caution about modern fly lines: Line makers are now selling some lines tailored to either cold-water conditions or warm-water conditions. You want to be sure that if you purchase one of these lines that it really fits your needs. A fly line constructed for cold-water fishing may tangle badly when used in the tropics, and lines for tropical or warm-water fishing will be unsuitable for colder waters.

Proper care of your fly lines will make them last for years. One manufacturer estimated that a line that is properly cared for should be good for at least 20,000 casts—which is a lot. I have lines that have been used fairly often that are 8 years old or older, and they still function well.

One of the greatest enemies of fly lines is heat. Never store your lines where they will be exposed to heat for long periods, such as in your car in the summer. Some sunscreens, most insect repellents, and other chemicals can damage a fly line. Try not to step on your fly line. Perhaps the fastest way to ruin a fly line is to scuff it or roll your foot over it on a boat deck to get it out of the way. This places kinks and coils in the line that interfere with fishing and are impossible to remove. Such lines may be repaired by cutting out the kinky portion of line and connecting the two good ends with the braided mono running line.

Good floating lines will float—so long as they are clean. It is the dirt that collects on a floating fly line that causes it to sink. There are a number of commercial line cleaners on the market, but the safest and least expensive way is to use warm water and soap, *not detergent*. I recommend a mild liquid soap, as for use on the skin. Wash the line with a sponge or rag. Then be sure that you remove all soap from the line with a thorough rinsing.

Some fishermen develop "ring" cracks in the first several feet of their fly line and assume it is a faulty line. Actually, it is poor casting technique. If the angler comes forward too soon on the forward cast, it actually cracks the line like a whip. This sudden acceleration simply deteriorates the coating on the fly line. The only way to prevent this is to delay the forward cast.

Reels

Unless you plan to fight giant tarpon or long-running offshore species such as tuna, billfish, and wahoo, you don't need to own a pricey reel that holds a huge amount of line.

For most inshore fishing (stripers, bluefish, seatrout, snook, redfish, jack crevalle, and similar species), a reel that holds 100 yards of backing is ample. Remember that a football field is 100 yards long. Add to that a 30-yard or longer fly line and you simply have more than enough line. For albacore and bonefish, you might make an exception and have a reel loaded with no more than 150 yards of backing, and that might be overly cautious.

You also don't need a reel that is capable of more than two pounds of drag pressure. Nothing on inshore waters will require more than a pound of drag. What you do need is a smooth drag. Hold a length six-pound monofilament between your two hands and slowly pull your hands apart, trying to break the line. You will find difficulty in doing so. But, if you jerk the hands apart, the line breaks easily. When fighting fish, the jerk is what breaks almost all leaders. If you can prevent jerking on the line, you will rarely break it. To eliminate jerking, you need a drag that allows line to slip smoothly from the spool. An easy way to check your drag is to run the line through the rod guides and attach a line end to a bicycle and have someone pedal off. Watch the rod tip. If the tip bounces up and down, you have an erratic drag that will probably lose your fish.

A good drag is usually made of one or more soft and hard washers. The hard ones are compressed against the spongy soft ones to obtain the correct resistance. One of the fastest ways to ruin a good drag is to adjust the drag and then leave it in that position. This eventually hardens the softer washers, which gives you an inferior drag. Release all drag pressure at the end of each fishing day to maintain a good drag.

There are a number of reels on the market today that cost less than $200 (some much less) that will subdue almost any inshore species you are likely to encounter.

Fly reels that have a small diameter require too many turns when recovering line. Try to buy a reel that has a spool width of at least three inches. This will allow you to recover line faster.

While fly reels designed for fresh water can be used, you will have to be careful and thoroughly cleanse them of salt residue after each use. Reels designed for saltwater use generally only need to have the outer surfaces washed lightly with warm soap and water. If the reel is cleaned well so that no dirt or oil remains, a coating of hard paste wax will ensure that the reel stays in good condition.

Knots and Leaders

There are hundreds of knots—some good, some better, and some very bad. Fortunately, a saltwater fly fisherman needs only a few. If you master the following knots, you can go anywhere in the world and make connections that will serve you well between your backing, line, leader, and fly.

The most important factor in building good knots—whether it is tying a 2-inch hawser to secure a ship to the dock or knotting a fragile 8X leader tippet to a size 22 dry fly—is that *no knot breaks until it begins to slip.* A poorly designed knot that has been closed very firmly will not fail as quickly as a well-designed knot that is not closed securely.

Lubricating monofilament helps secure the knot better. You can use spittle or water. It is not advisable to use silicone or some other slippery substance. Although these certainly help the coils to close easier as you tighten them, they may also allow the tag end to slither through and cause the knot to fall apart. Tying an overhand knot in the tag end to prevent it from slipping is not a good fix, because either the knot was a poor one in the first place or it was closed poorly. There are some glues on the market that are especially designed to be used with nylon monofilament, and these special glues will enhance knot strength. However, most of the cyanoacrylate glues are water soluble—something to remember.

It is extremely important to follow instructions carefully when tying a knot. The number of turns you make around the standing line is especially critical. Many tests were conducted to determine how many turns should be made with the tag end in a variety of knots. If a knot calls for four turns, and you make three, there are not enough turns around the standing line to keep the knot from slipping. If you make five turns, you may not be able to close the knot firmly enough to prevent it from slipping.

Another factor is how well the coils within the knot are closed. Never overlap a coil: A knot will break under severe strain where a coil overlaps. If the coils lay perfectly together, a knot will remain strong. But if a coil crosses over another during closure, the knot will break there under stress. Too many fishermen make this mistake.

Laboratory experiments show that when tying knots with monofilament stronger than 15-pound test, it is very difficult to secure the knot to its full potential with bare hands. Use gloves or pliers to ensure proper closure.

Fly fishermen frequently join monofilament of different diameters to build tapered leaders and to secure bite or shock tippets to a thinner tippet. These knots will close easier and better if you use monofilaments that are the same apparent limpness. If you use hard or stiff monofilament and try to tie it to mono that is more limp, the knot is very difficult to close well.

You may have been using a good knot for years. When someone shows you a new knot and claims that it's better than the knot you've been using for years, you can perform a simple test to determine which knot is better. Take two hooks from the same box. Tie your favorite knot to one hook and the new knot to the other. Take two pairs of pliers, grip each hook, and slowly pull them apart until one breaks. Repeat this test ten times to be sure.

You need to conduct one other test. Some knots, such as the Spider Hitch, are great knots for a slow, steady pull, but fail miserably if a jerk occurs. To test any knot properly, you need to check it both for steady pulls and quick jerks. Tie your favorite knot in another strand of mono and the new knot in the other end. Grasp each end with pliers and jerk them until a knot fails. Repeat this ten times. If you have tied both knots carefully each time, you will have a conclusive test as to which knot is stronger.

Finally, if you want to tie knots well, you need to practice them at home. Few fly fishermen do this. Tying a knot over and over at home will develop good technique so that your knots are as strong as possible. It will also improve your speed of operation. This allows you to catch more fish, because when your fly is not in the water, you're not catching fish.

The following are the knots I believe will let you fly fish with confidence in salt water anywhere in the world.

Knots

Whipped Loop

The Whipped Loop connection has a number of uses. It can connect leaders to fly lines, backing to fly lines, and shooting heads to shooting line. I much prefer the whipped loop to any other connection for attaching a leader to a fly line. Loops never hang up in the guides, going in or out. Most importantly, there are many occasions when you should change the leader on your line. If you're bonefishing in shallow water on a calm morning, you may need a leader that is 12 feet or longer to prevent frightening the fish. If the wind picks up, you may have trouble straightening a 12-foot leader, and because the surface is rippled, you can use a much shorter leader. With a Whipped Loop, you can easily replace the 12-foot leader with a new one. Some people will use a Nail Knot to attach a short length of monofilament and a Nail Knot in the tag end of the mono. This practice has never made sense to me, because heavy monofilament tends to drown the front end of a floating fly line, and it wears out quickly. And if you want a loop, why not just install it in the fly line? With a little practice, you can build a strong Whipped Loop in less than 30 seconds, which is less time than it would take to install a section of monofilament with a loop in the end.

Tube Nail Knot

The Tube Nail Knot is perhaps the most commonly used connection to attach a leader to a fly line. It is easy to tie, and when made properly, it is a strong connection. It also flows well through the guides if it is trimmed correctly and the knot is tapered smoothly with glue.

Joe Brooks, famed outdoor writer of the 1950s and '60s, discovered this knot while fishing in Argentina. The natives used a tapered horseshoe nail to make the knot, hence the name. When Joe wrote about the knot in *Outdoor Life,* it was a revelation in comparison with the various crude knots in use at the time.

There were tying problems encountered when using the nail, so someone came up with the idea of using a tube (see illustration on page 33). The neat thing about using a tube is that it reduces the diameter of the coils when making the knot. These coils need to be closed firmly after the nail or tube has been extracted. The smaller the tube, the less trouble you will encounter when drawing the coils tight.

The Nail Knot is also valuable because you can install it at any point on your fly line. For night fishing, you may want to place a knot where you would normally make a pickup for a backcast. For clear lines, such as those made from monofilament, it's advisable to place a nail knot where you can best lift the line from the water to backcast.

Whipped Loop

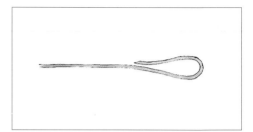

Use a fly-tying bobbin with high-quality size A thread. Feed the thread and detach the spool. Wrap the spool four times around one leg of the bobbin to maintain the correct amount of tension. Form the loop with the last two inches of the fly line.

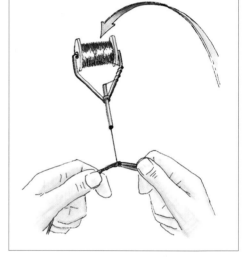

Lay the tag ends of the fly line and thread together, and wrap the thread on as you would when you tie a fly. When it is secure, grip the loop in your right hand and the fly line and tag end in your left hand, and rotate your hands so that the thread wraps deeply into the line. Try to lay the wraps down neatly.

Taper the tag end of the fly line with a razor and wrap the thread past the tag end. The total length of the wrapping should be about ½ inch and no more than ¾ inch. Make a loop of 4- or 10-pound test mono and wrap over the loop about ten times, as shown.

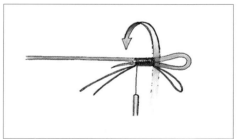

Cut the thread from the bobbin and place the tag end of the thread in the mono loop. Then pull the tag ends of the mono loop until it draws the tag end of the thread under the ten wraps. Carefully trim the tag end of the thread.

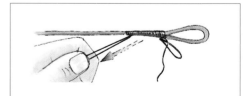

Coat the wraps with a rubber-based cement such as Pliobond and test the loops. If the threads were not buried deeply enough in the line, the loop will pull out.

Tube Nail Knot

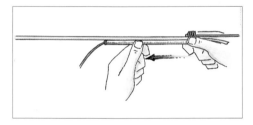

Lay a short hollow tube along the tag end of the fly line as shown. Place the butt section of the leader alongside the tube and fly line. The tag end of the leader should be about twelve inches long and should be to the left, as shown.

Hold the tube, fly line, and leader tightly between your thumb and forefinger. Wrap the tag end of the leader against the tube, line, and standing end of the leader. Keep the wraps from unraveling with your thumb and forefinger, and lay each wrap closely against the last. Make six to eight wraps.

Insert the tag end of leader through the hollow tube.

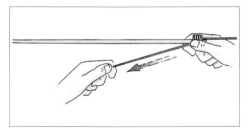

Carefully switch hands so that the coils don't unravel and pull the tag end through the tube. Then pull the tube out from your right thumb and forefinger as you grip the coil tightly.

Keeping the pressure on the coils, pull gently on the tag end of the leader until the coils begin to tighten. Carefully slide the wraps toward the tag end as you tighten the knot. Pull on the standing end of the leader and the tag end to finally tighten the knot.

Trim the tag end of the leader and the tag end of the fly line, if any. The finished Tube Nail Knot should look like this.

Surgeon's Knot

A Surgeon's Knot is used to connect two different diameters of line. Of course, it can be used to connect two lines of the same diameter, but it can also connect braided wire to monofilament, something many fishermen don't realize. For many, the Surgeon's Knot is the preferred knot for building tapered leaders. When properly tied, it has a knot strength exceeding 90 percent of the weaker of the lines used in the connection. I consider this to be a knot *every* fisherman should know.

The most important factor in building this knot to retain maximum strength is that *all four ends of the knot must be firmly pulled tight after closure.*

Bimini Twist

The Bimini Twist is the most important knot that a saltwater fly fisherman can learn, but it has applications in fresh water, too. Whenever you want to connect a fragile line to another line and retain 100 percent of the strength of the fragile line, you must use a Bimini Twist. Many fishermen do not understand why this knot is so valuable, but there are almost no other knots that offer full line strength. In most cases, if you tie a knot to a swivel, hook, or other device, the knot will usually be weaker than the line it is tied with.

The Bimini Twist is a wrapping in the line that is stronger than the line itself. Most important, it is a loop (or two strands) that is used to tie the knot. Because the Bimini Twist is stronger than the line, and you are tying the knot with two strands of the line, almost any connection will be stronger than the main line. This is why the Bimini is used throughout the fishing world, from big-game trolling to fishing with a 4-pound fly tippet.

Albright Special

There are many knots used to connect two diameters of monofilament that differ considerably in diameter. The most useful of these is the Albright Special. The Huffnagle is a modern knot that does the same thing, but it is limited to use only with monofilament. The Albright can be used to join mono to mono, mono to braided wire, mono to solid wire, a butt section to a fly line, and backing to the fly line (although there are better knots for the last two purposes).

In making an Albright, it is important to never cross one wrap over the other as the knot is being built. This is where the knot will break under great stress.

Surgeon's Knot

Lay the two lines together as shown, overlapping each other about six inches.

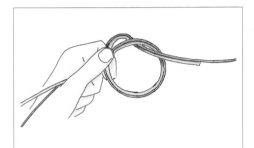

Make an overhand knot, and keep the loop open.

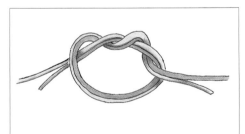

Pass the line and leader through the loop again.

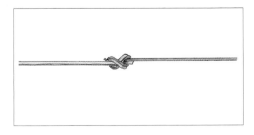

Moisten the knot. Hold the tag ends and standing ends, and carefully tighten the knot. It is important to pull all four ends simultaneously and as tightly as possible.

Trim the tag ends.

Bimini Twist

Make a loop in the line around your right hand—there should be about four feet of tag line—and wrap the tag line twenty times around the standing line.

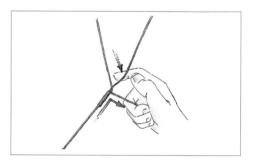

Place the loop on your knee. Draw the twists tight by pulling the standing line and the tag line toward you and then drawing your hands apart. The angle that the tag line and standing line make should not exceed 90 degrees.

To tie the knot successfully, you must maintain the 90-degree angle between the standing line and the tag line. Move the standing line and tag line simultaneously to the left so that the standing line is straight and the tag line is now 90 degrees to the right. Pull on the standing line and ease the tag end in your right hand until the tag end jumps the first twist. Feed the tag end gradually toward the twists until the spiral wraps continue toward the beginning of the loop.

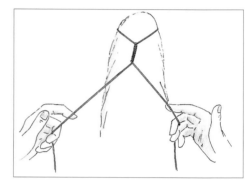

Without relaxing the tension on the standing line, slide your left hand down and grip the last spiral wrap with your left thumb and forefinger. Pass the tag end around one end of the loop, as shown, and back through the new loop. Pull the loop tight, work it toward the wraps, and pull it tight until it locks. You should now be able to let go of the knot and take it off your knee.

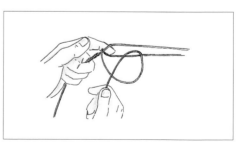

(continued)

Bimini Twist *(continued)*

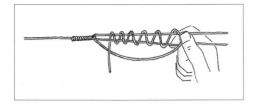

Hold the two legs of the loop with your right hand. Pass the tag end over the loop about two inches to the right of the spiral wraps. Wrap the tag end around the two legs of the loop four times from right to left toward the spiral wraps.

Pull the tag end and work the new spirals back toward the first spiral wraps. This should take a few tugs of the tag end. Tug and work the spirals back until they lock on to the Bimini Twist.

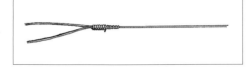

Carefully trim the tag end.

Albright Special

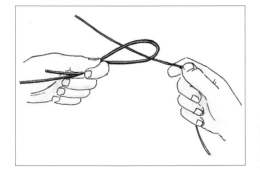

Bend a loop in the tag end of the heavier line or mono. Insert ten inches of the tag end of the lighter line through the loop and grip it with your left thumb and forefinger.

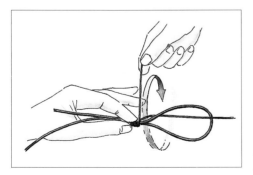

Wrap the tag end of the lighter line from left to right ten to twelve times over the two strands of the loop and the standing line of the lighter line. Wrap each loop closely to the last, carefully covering the wraps with your thumb and forefinger.

(continued)

Albright Special *(continued)*

Insert the tag end through the loop so that it exits the loop through the same side that it entered. Hold the wraps with the left thumb and forefinger and pull the standing line.

Push the wraps toward the loop as you pull on the standing line. Be careful not to push the wraps over the end of the loop. You can use a pair of pliers to pull the standing line of the smaller line.

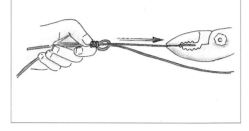

Pull on the standing lines of both the heavier and the lighter lines until the knot tightens.

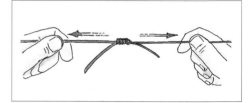

Loop the tag end of the smaller line over its standing line, then make three wraps as shown.

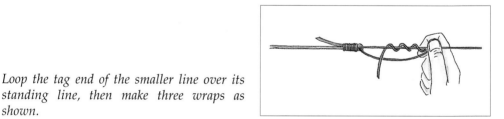

Pull on the tag end.

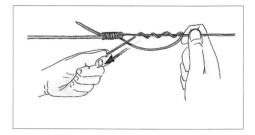

Trim the tag ends of both lines.

Nonslip Loop

The Nonslip Loop is an old knot that I worked with for months before finally improving it. It is the strongest loop knot possible. I now use this knot more than any other to connect monofilament leaders to flies. To obtain maximum strength, the knot must be tied correctly—the correct number of turns must be made with the tag end around the standing line. It can be tied with line of any diameter—from 8X to 150-pound monofilament to braided wire—and you can adjust the size of the loop. It is superb for making a loop in your tapered leader or to connect a tippet to the leader.

There are many fishing situations for which a loop knot is desirable. Anytime a heavy tippet is connected to a smaller fly, the junction between the two can impede the action of the fly. Popping Bugs, for example, are much more effective when you attach them with a free-swinging loop. A fly like the Clouser Minnow will be much more alive on the retrieve, as will almost any underwater fly.

Some people use the Uni-knot for this connection. Certainly this is sufficient, but the Uni-knot is not nearly as strong a knot as the Nonslip Loop, and the Uni-knot often slips down and tightens on the eye of a hook when it's under tension. The Nonslip Loop retains its shape regardless of fishing conditions.

Figure-8 Knot

A Figure-8 Knot is the *only* knot used to attach braided wire to a swivel or hook eye. It should never be used to tie nylon monofilament—the knot will slip or fail miserably. But it is incredibly simple for use with braided wire and has excellent knot strength.

Aside from tying it correctly, the most important factor when making this knot is how you draw it tight. Never pull on the standing line to close the knot. This will feed kinked line in front of the fly, which will cause it to wobble erratically on the retrieve. Carefully draw out all slack within the knot as you pull on the tag end. That way all kinks in the line can be clipped and discarded.

Backing Tips

Backing is often ignored when fly tackle is considered, but it forms a vital link between you and a trophy fish, and it deserves your attention. This does not apply just to saltwater situations. Steelheaders often watch in dismay as a fish escapes downstream, where they can't follow, only to see the end of the backing—and the fight. Atlantic salmon fishermen often have to give more line than they'd like to a battling fish. Even on light gear, a good trout hooked in heavy water may run more than a 90-foot length of fly line.

Nonslip Loop

Make an overhand knot, but do not tighten it completely. Pass the tag end through the hook or lure. Pass the tag end back through the overhand knot, as shown, making sure to pass it through the same part of the loop it entered.

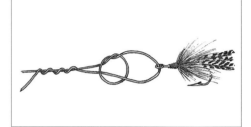

Wrap the tag end seven times for 8X to 6-pound test, five times for 8- to 12-pound test, four times for 15- to 45-pound test, three times for 50- to 60-pound test, and two times for 70-pound test or heavier.

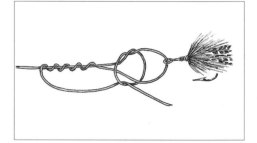

Insert the tag end back through the end of the overhand knot as shown.

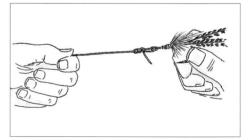

Moisten the knot and tighten it by pulling the tag end, the standing line, and the two legs of the loop.

Figure-8 Knot

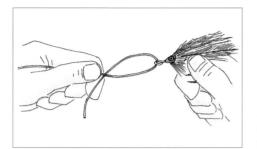

Pass the tag end through the eye of the hook and form a loop by passing the line under the standing line.

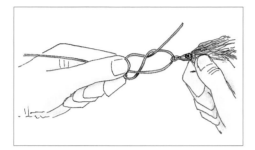

Pass the tag end over the standing line and back through the first loop.

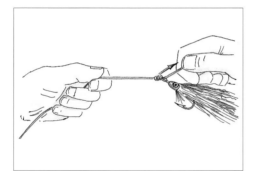

Tighten the knot by pulling on the tag end with a pair of pliers. Trim the tag end, but leave a sufficient amount to be able to undo the knot.

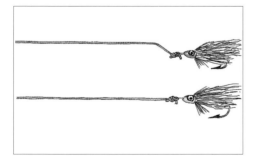

Do not tighten the knot by pulling on the standing end—it will form a bend in the standing end as in the upper illustration.

Fly lines are rarely longer than 105 feet—a very short run for some freshwater and certainly many saltwater species. To allow fish to make long runs and exhaust themselves, there has to be enough backing on the reel so that the best fish you hope to hook can be landed. But you shouldn't use just any backing. The type of backing used, the length, and sometimes the color can all play important factors in catching fish.

There are a number of lines used for backing. Nylon monofilament is rarely used, because it stretches when pulled taut. For example, if you are fighting a strong fish with mono backing and you recover some of this line on the reel, it will be in a stretched condition. Then, piling loose line on top of it may create a critical problem. The fish makes another long run, comes to the stretched portion (so that it is now thinner mono and it has dug into the bed of line), and a jerk occurs as mono feeds up to the embedded line. This will often snap your leader.

The most popular backing is Dacron, available in most tackle shops, or a very similar material called Micron. These lines owe their popularity to the fact that they stretch very little under stress, and both lines lies flat on the spool.

The ultrathin braided casting lines appear to be a breakthrough in fly-reel backing. But there are some drawbacks to these lines. They are often referred to as gel-spun Spectra or braided polyethylene lines. Stren manufactures a slightly different line using Kevlar; others use various braiding systems and materials. These lines are unlike any other Dacron, Micron, braided nylon, or nylon lines. They are a totally new breed of lines. Their outstanding characteristics are that they are thin and strong.

The average new braided casting line of 30 pounds has the diameter of about a 10-pound nylon monofilament line. You may think that you can put two or three times as much line on a reel as you do now, but I believe you will encounter difficulties if you use any of these braided lines testing *less than 30 pounds* (for larger fish, I recommend 50-pound test) for backing. Lines testing less than 30 pounds are so thin that they tend to dig into the backing, which causes the same kind of problems associated with nylon monofilament. Many of these lines are round and very slick. If you fail to carefully wind the line level back on the reel spool as you recover it while fighting a fish, it tends to pile higher on one side of the spool and tumble into a disastrous mess.

You will also need special knots to tie most of the braided casting lines—conventional knots usually are poor performers. If you want to connect a monofilament leader to one of these braided lines, use the Braided Line Connection Knot shown here.

If you do use these new braided lines for backing on fly reels, the most important factor in getting good performance is how the line is placed on the spool. The diameter of the 30-pound test is so thin that you must make sure that all the backing is put on the reel as firmly as possible. I use a glove to put tension on the line as I reel it on the spool. If you fail to do this, even 30-pound test may dig into the backing and cause a lost fish.

Braided Line Connection Knot

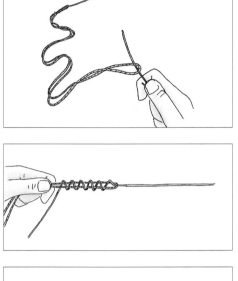

Put a Bimini Twist in the braided line. Pass one to two feet of tag line of the wire through the loop.

Wrap the wire around the braided Bimini loop six times.

Wrap the wire back over the spiral wraps made in the previous step and pass the tag end through the Bimini loop, exiting through the end that the tag end entered.

Draw the wire tight and place five barrel wraps around the standing line of the wire.

These new braided lines (of approximately 30-pound test) have advantages fly fishermen may consider. If you fish offshore, where your fish may run a long distance, a huge belly can develop in the line. This belly causes tremendous drag on the leader and may break it. Because the polyethylene lines have almost no stretch, the line does not belly and you remain in as close as possible contact with the fish.

For saltwater fly fishermen, the angler who will carefully install the backing properly on the spool can add about 50 percent more backing than if Dacron or Micron is used. For anglers who prefer the smaller saltwater reels (for example, when bonefishing), you can now fish with the proper fly line and adequate backing. And, for those who seek long-running fish, such as billfish, you will be able to put more backing on a reel formerly loaded with Dacron or Micron.

It is worth realizing that when backing was the cause of a lost fish, in the majority of these cases, the reason was improper installation of the backing. Regardless of whether you are using Dacron, Micron, or a new braided casting line, it is extremely important that the backing be placed on the spool under pressure so that the bedding is firm and will not allow the backing to dig into itself.

The two most often used backing lines are 20- to 30-pound test Dacron or Micron. The size of the reel spool (if it is small, you can't get very much 30-pound test line on it) and the strength of the leader tippet are factors that determine which test should be used. Obviously, you don't want to use backing weaker than the tippet. If the backing breaks, you may lose leader, line, and fish.

If you fish for seatrout, bonefish, redfish, and other species that don't require a heavy leader tippet and prefer small, light reels, you may be tempted to select 20-pound test Dacron or Micron. However, I use 30-pound Dacron or Micron for almost all my backing needs on fly reels because it is much less susceptible to abrasion.

Another mistake many longtime fly fishermen make is to never replace backing. Abusive conditions can ruin even new backing. For example, if you are fishing a coral-studded flat and a fish makes along run, the line and backing will be dragged over the sharp rocks and nicked or frayed. It pays to check your backing routinely.

Backing on fly reels gives the fish enough line to make an escape run. For years, outdoor writers and fly fishermen have vastly overrated the distance that many fish will run. Bluefish and stripers will rarely run into more than 125 yards of backing. I've caught a number of large stripers, as well as bluefish to 18 pounds on fly—none ever hit 100 yards of backing plus fly line.

Bonefish are legendary and supposed to run 250 yards. I have caught quite a few heavier than 10 pounds, but none ran farther than a fly line and 150 yards of backing. (If you included the fly line and leader, that is already nearly two football fields away!) Many fly fishermen who seek snook, redfish, seatrout, and similar species carry reels loaded with 250 to 300 yards of backing, but it will never be needed.

There are some fishing situations for which a lot of backing is demanded. You'll need a lot of line (at least 300 to 400 yards) for billfish and some of the offshore speedsters, such as wahoo, tuna, and mackerel exceeding 40 pounds. Giant tarpon can pull a lot of backing from a reel, especially if you are fighting from a staked or anchored boat. But with these few exceptions, a fly fisherman who has a reel loaded with 150 yards of backing and a fly line will almost never hook a fish in his or her lifetime that will ever run that far.

There are several techniques concerning backing that anglers have devised that you may want to consider.

Colors

Some anglers have fly line and backing that are a similar color. That is not a good idea! I prefer to connect a backing that is markedly different in color from the rear of the fly line to indicate the end of the fly line.

It is often advantageous to know just how much line has been pulled from the reel. For example, if you are on a saltwater flat and you know there is a marker or channel buoy 200 yards away, you must know how much line the fish has pulled out.

Backing comes in many colors, ranging from fluorescent colors to dull reddish-brown. Some anglers will use various lengths of different colors to tip them off. For example, you may connect 100 feet of bright chartreuse backing to the fly line. The next 100 feet would be a much different color, and so on. Use loops to connect the line. Bimini Twists can be made in both ends of each color of backing and they can be looped together. Many fly shops can also build blind-spliced loops in your backing if you don't know how. The loops will flow through the guides, and if at any time you want to add or remove a color link, simply unloop it.

Shock Absorbers

Billfish and tarpon jump frequently and make lunges against the leader. Many experienced anglers take pride in scorning any effort to reduce the shock against the fly or leader of a leaping fish. However, for fishermen who only occasionally encounter these jumpers, there is a way of building a shock absorber into the backing that will reduce the chance of a leaping fish breaking the leader or ripping the fly loose. Connect 100 feet of 25- or 30-pound brightly colored nylon monofilament with a Bimini Twist Loop to the rear of the fly line. Then connect the other end of the nylon monofilament to your backing with a loop-to-loop system. If a fish jumps and you have the fly line and the monofilament outside the rod tip, the mono will stretch like a giant rubber band, which will prevent the leader from snapping. You want brightly colored monofilament so that a boat operator can see it during the battle and they won't run over it—something that has happened to me.

Maintenance

Modern saltwater fly reels require little maintenance, and one area that almost never receives attention is the backing. If you fought a fish that ran well into the backing, it will have soaked up a lot of salt water. After the long run, the backing line is recovered. When you get home the reel surfaces are cleaned. But the salt-encrusted backing is generally left untouched. I recommend that you fill a sink with warm soapy water and feed the backing into it. Wash the spool sides with the same soapy water and wipe it clean. Drain the soapy water, flush the backing line with clean water, and replace it firmly on the spool.

You need to securely connect the backing to the reel spool axle. The Uniknot is suitable, and the arbor knot rarely fails, but it is weaker. Once the backing is securely fastened to the spool axle and the backing is firmly installed on the reel, the fly line needs to be connected.

Connecting Fly Line to Backing

First, let's examine the criteria for a proper backing/fly line connection. I would recommend a knot that is easy to disconnect so that you can easily exchange one line for another. Any knot should be as strong as the backing, or very close to its strength, and it must be able to pass smoothly through the guides and tip-top, both while paying out and returning. Some knots pass smoothly through the guide when traveling in one direction, but not in the other direction. Two good examples of such a connection are the Albright and the Nail Knot. With the Albright, the fly line is folded over in a horseshoe shape to connect the backing to it. One leg of the Albright is the stub of the fly line. Unless this stub is coated with something to create a smooth joint, it can catch on a guide or tip-top as the fish pulls the knot through. A Nail Knot has a stub, and unless a smooth coating is placed over it, on returning to the reel the stub can catch in the guides.

My personal choice for a connection to the backing loop is the Whipped Loop, which allows you to change lines quickly. When properly constructed, this loop is stronger than the fly line, and because it is rounded as it passes in and out of the guides, it is a trouble-free knot. I urge you to try the Whipped Loop. With a little practice, it can be made in less than 2 minutes.

Another connection favored by some experienced anglers is the Double Nail Knot Loop. There is a chance that a small protruding stub may be formed when the knot is finished. A smooth joint can be made (also with the Albright Knot) by coating it with Goop, Pliobond, Aqua-Seal, or another flexible glue. Use enough to form a taper on both sides of the knot so that it resembles a football shape.

Marking Lines

It is a scene that is repeated constantly by saltwater fly fishermen who fish from boats. The fisherman stands in the bow of a flats skiff, strips off line, takes out the tangles, makes a cast, and stands ready for whatever comes along. The guide spots a really nice fish. Excited, the angler false casts and directs the fly to the fish. All too often, the cast is ruined because he was standing on the line, or perhaps the cast may have been perfect and the fish was hooked, but when the fish took off, the line was underfoot or tangled on something inside the boat. Another lost opportunity. If you're a fly fisherman, I'm sure these things have happened to you.

Double Nail Knot Loop

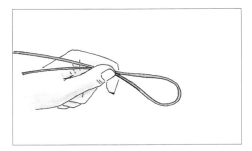

Form a loop at the end of the fly line.

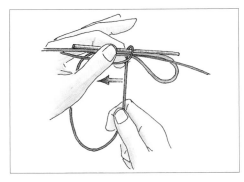

Place a paper clip on the loop, and place a piece of looped mono underneath, as shown. The tag end of the mono is to the left. Wrap the right-hand part of the mono loop closely over the line loop, standing end of the mono, and the paper clip five times, from right to left.

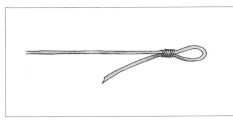

Trim the tag end and standing line of the mono.

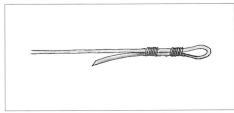

Place an identical Nail Knot behind the first.

Coat both knots with Pliobond.

Such disasters can be prevented. The problem is that most fly fishermen pull off too much line. Just because you bought a 100-foot fly line doesn't mean you have to pull it all off to be ready. Instead, you should only pull of the amount of line needed for the existing condition. If you plan to cast along a shoreline and the longest cast is maybe 45 feet, don't pull off more line. If you are throwing at stripers and you can only cast 50 feet, stripping out any more line is just asking for trouble.

Once the problem is understood, how do you know the correct amount of line to strip from the reel? There is an easy solution. Pull off the amount of line you can normally cast or would use. When you've established the length, make a 1-foot-long mark with a permanent black pen. You need to make this indicator prominent, so it is easily seen, and a mark of at least 1 foot stands out. Once you know the amount that you can cast, you can keep the rest of the line on your reel and eliminate most of the above-mentioned problems. This mark will last for the life of the fly line.

There is another problem that frustrates even good fly fishermen, yet there is a simple answer. Today, many lines are of a single color. With sinking lines, you make a cast, the fly and line sink well below the surface, and then you begin your retrieve. Because the line is a single color throughout its length, or if it is clear monofilament, you don't know when to pick up for a backcast. If you pick up too soon, you can't get the line out of the water for a good backcast. If you retrieve too much line, several false casts have to be made to work out enough line to make the forward cast.

Again, you must mark the fly line to match your skill. Take a marking pen and go to some water. Make a number of casts to determine where you can comfortably pick up this line for a backcast and make a mark where your hand holds the line before backcasting. Take the line home and make a ten-turn Nail Knot on the line at the mark with 8-pound test monofilament. Once the knot has been installed at the correct place on the fly line, close it firmly. Trim the two ends smoothly and then coat the knot with Pliobond (a rubber-based glue), Goop, or similar cement. When you retrieve line, you don't have to think about when you should make the pickup for a backcast. When you feel the nail knot bump over your finger, you'll know it's time to lift the line from the water.

There is another line-marking trick that has been a great help to me since the 1960s. Almost anyone who has been fly fishing very long has several lines in different sizes, especially if you fish bass, trout, and salt water. The labels that come with a new fly line often fall off and then it can be difficult to know the line's size.

Fortunately, there is an easy labeling system. Grab that now-familiar black marking pen. A 1-inch-long mark that encircles the fly line is a number five, and a small ring made with the marker around the line indicates the number one. Thus, if you have a 1-inch mark followed by three small rings, you have an 8-weight line.

A weight-forward fly line has most of the large diameter concentrated at the front. Place the large mark at the front end and the smaller rings behind.

If you have a dark-colored line, on which the black marker pen would not show, you have another option. Purchase shrink tubing at an electrical store. Cut the shrink tubing to a 1-inch length for a number five and small rings for ones. Slip them through the line, hold them in position, and then dip them in boiling water. A brief immersion won't hurt the fly line, and the tubing will shrink and firmly secure itself to the line.

Leaders

A leader has three functions. First, it puts a near-invisible connection between the fly and the line. Second, it allows the fly to move freely; if you attached the fly directly to the fly line, little action would occur. Third, and most important, it keeps the fly line well back from the fly so that fish aren't disturbed by the line when it hits the water or by the line's shadow.

There are three parts to most leaders. The butt section is usually the largest in diameter and is attached to the fly line. The midsection connects the butt section to the thinnest part, called the tippet.

It is important to understand how the leader delivers the fly at the end of the cast. When your rod stops on the forward cast, the line begins to unroll toward the target. After the entire line has unrolled, the leader must also unroll to make the cast. If it doesn't, the fly and line might splash down all at once, which may spook a fish. If the butt section is too weak or thin, the leader cannot continue to unroll, and the leader will collapse. If stiff butt material is used, it actually resists unrolling, and poor delivery results.

I suggest that you learn to make your own tapered saltwater leaders, because you need to adjust them for different conditions. The leader should be constructed from various diameters of monofilament all from the same brand. It is not as important to use a particular brand as it is to use mono from the same manufacturer, because the different line tests are more uniform in limpness within the same brand. Use premium or top-of-the-line spinning line. *The butt section must be one-half the length of the entire leader. This will ensure that energy flowing through the line will help the leader to continue to unroll.*

Here is a chart that will help you make your own leaders. Bear in mind that you can be inches off on any of the segments and the leader will still work fine. There is no need for a micrometer—just use the same brand of premium monofilament. If you are throwing heavy wind-resistant flies or using a line size 9 or larger, I would suggest starting the butt section with 50-pound monofilament. If you are using flies that are smaller and easier to cast or rods size 9 or smaller, then you can start the butt section with 40-pound test. The tippet on any tapered leader will usually range from 18 to 24 inches.

The following table gives specifications for building leaders with a butt section of 50 pounds. If you use a 40-pound butt section, adjust accordingly.

Length	50 lb.	40 lb.	30 lb.	20 lb.	15–12–10 lb.
8 feet	4'	1"	6"	6"	1½–2'
9 feet	4½'	1'	1'	6"	1½–2'
10 feet	5'	1'	1'	1'	2'
12 feet	6'	2'	1'	1'	2'
14 feet	7'	3'	1'	1'	2'
16 feet	8'	4'	1'	1'	2'

C H A P T E R   5

Flies

Many newcomers to saltwater fly fishing ask if there is a basic list of effective flies that they can use in most waters, under most conditions, most of the time. The simple answer is yes, but before I suggest the basic patterns, I want to caution that you do not necessarily have to use these flies. There are many flies that work. Some people may feel that the following list is incomplete because their favorite fly isn't mentioned here, but I'm confident that the following suggestions will do the job most of the time in most of the places you fish. It is important to realize, however, that you may need to alter the amount of dressing, the color combinations, or size to be most effective under local conditions.

Basic Considerations

Before listing the flies, I would like to present some basics to consider when choosing a fly.

Depth

The sink rate of any fly you cast is important. You will need flies that work on the surface, ones that work just under the surface, some that fish a little deeper, and a few that dive well down in the water column. The weight of a hook shank can be critical. Standard-weight shanks are used most often. However, there are times when an extra-heavy shank aids in getting the fly to sink deeper.

Length

The length of a fly is often critical. For example, striped bass will sometimes feed on baitfish of a specific size. If the flies you are casting don't exactly match the color, but closely match the length, you can draw many strikes. This is especially the case when many species have pushed the baitfish to the surface and are gorging on them. Consider, too, that some fish, such as bonefish and redfish, have relatively small mouths. Therefore, a 5-inch fly might occasionally catch fish with small mouths, but shorter flies are a more attractive offering.

Structure

If you fly fish in salt water, you realize the value of being able to retrieve your fly through weeds, boat docks, and rock piles without having it snag. Vegetation can also be a problem in some saltwater situations. Floating grass, aquatic grasses growing on the bottom, and a shoreline housing mangroves and other line-catching structure will require a weedless fly. The trouble is that weedless flies are often fishless flies. The hooks on some flies are bent so that they won't snag unwanted matter, but these hooks are often very difficult to set when a fish strikes.

A number of products have been used to make weedless flies. The most common material is a hard or extra-stiff monofilament. This works well for a while, but after a few fish chew on it, the monofilament becomes so battered and misshapen that it is useless, and it must be clipped from the pattern. Solid trolling wire is sometimes better, because its stiffness offers excellent resistance to weeds, but the wire bends out of shape easily. If you try to reshape it, the wire will probably break. If it doesn't break, then it is usually impossible to reform to the original weed guard.

So what can we do about it? That's a question I worried over for some years. I wanted something that was easy to obtain. It had to be durable, so that a lot of fish could chew on the fly and the guard would still be usable. It had to be easy to attach to the fly. Finally, if it did bend out of shape, it had to be easily reformed.

I now use 30- or 40-pound-test plastic-coated stainless steel braided wire. This is usually placed in front of a fly for barracuda or bluefish and other toothy critters. If you buy a package of commercial steel leaders, they will probably be made from this material. This wire is generally composed of seven or more very fine strands. The braided wire is then coated with a tough, supple plastic. Don't use the uncoated wire because the end will untwist and make a useless weed guard.

I am using the conventional plastic-coated braided wire, not the material that has appeared the past several years on the market that is super thin. This newer and thinner wire is not stiff enough for weed guards. The approximate diameter of the older wire I use is .030 inch.

Each manufacturer has different colors of plastic coating on their wires. I have tried light tan, dark brown, and black, and I can see no difference in strike ratio. However, I have not used the very black wire for a guard on streamer flies made of pale synthetics, such as the Sand Lance. I think that nickel-plated or stainless hooks on many flies are appropriate if the pattern imitates a silver-colored minnow, and for that reason I don't use black wire—it seems to stand out too much.

Color

A good rule when seeking bottom-feeding fish, such as redfish and bonefish, is to start with flies that match the color of the bottom. Common sense tells us that any creature whose color contrasts with the bottom on which it lives will have been easily seen and eaten eons ago. However, an exception seems to be using flies that have chartreuse in the wing. Nobody knows why this is one of the most effective colors in saltwater fly fishing.

Wing Materials

When you fish unusually clear waters, opaque wing materials, such as bucktail, are often not as productive as translucent synthetics. This was a major reason why translucent polar bear hair, now illegal to use, was coveted as wing material in streamer flies.

Hooks

Let's consider some of the requirements for saltwater fly-fishing hooks. First, bronze hooks are not recommended because they rust quickly. Instead, use plated hooks or stainless steel hooks. The Mustad 34007 (regular length shank) and the longer-shank Mustad 34011 have been the most popular stainless hooks for many years. These stainless hooks are not as sharp, nor do they possess the strength of other hooks, but flies tied on these hooks have landed fish successfully for many years around the globe.

Size is also important. Many saltwater fly fishermen use hooks that are far too large. Freshwater anglers can catch large trout on a size 22 hook, but the same anglers will use a size 2/0 for a saltwater fish that is hardly much bigger. Many experienced *tarpon* fishermen now use a 2/0—or at the most, a 3/0—for giant tarpon of more than 140 pounds. In fact, there are few big saltwater fish that can't be landed on a 2/0 hook.

Despite this, many striped bass anglers favor 3/0 to 5/0 hooks. The major disadvantage to using these larger hooks is that they are much more difficult to cast.

Large hooks also have a thicker wire diameter, which makes them more difficult to set on strikes. The difference between casting a pattern dressed on a size 1/0 and one dressed on a 4/0 is astounding. If a fish has large mouth, like a striped bass does, large hooks are not necessary, because the fish doesn't bite the fly. Instead, it opens its cavernous mouth and inhales the fly. I have caught a number of stripers between 20 and 30 pounds on a size 2/0 fly, which is the largest that I recommend.

Flies tied on very small hooks, such as a size 8, will certainly interest bonefish. But a big bone is a hard-running fish, and such a small hook often dislodges because doesn't hold enough flesh. I like to use a size 4 or 2 hook for most of my bonefish flies.

Points and Barbs

Modern hooks have very small barbs, which are recommended. I have been hooked by a number of people, and a little bit of barb holds a lot of meat. You need almost no barb to hold a fish during a fight. In fact, I have been using barbless hooks since 1956 and can't detect any difference in success with or without barbs on hooks. Many anglers fear that they will lose fish if there is no barb. I strongly urge everyone to use barbless hooks.

When selecting saltwater hooks, look at the points. If they are long and narrow, avoid them. Many saltwater fish have tough mouths, and a long, thin point will often curl when you set it in a fish, even if it is well sharpened.

Flash Materials

The use of flash materials is often detrimental when seeking some species, but in most cases (especially if you are imitating baitfish), adding flash will draw more strikes. The trend in flash materials has been to use thinner material and softer or more flexible flash. A combination of several colors of flash usually results in a more effective fly, because few things in nature are a single color.

Whenever you build a fly of red and white, it will be more effective if the wing is all white and the red portion is very short and located at the front. I believe that attacking fish see the bait with a long white belly and red gills at the front. Experience has shown that decreasing the red portion of the wing results in more strikes.

Eyes

Many fly patterns are tied without eyes. But there are frequent fishing situations in which the eyes can make a difference between success and failure. Some baitfish have actually evolved to have a pattern on the rear of their body that resembles a huge eye. If the baitfish is facing south and a predator moves in to capture it, the predator thinks the baitfish is going to flee to the north because of the false eye pattern on the rear of its body. Instead, the baitfish flees in the opposite direction.

There is no doubt in my mind that predatory fish concentrate on the eye of the prey just before striking. Experiments in clear water have convinced me that fly patterns with eyes are more effective at drawing attention and strikes from predatory fish and that flies with enlarged or exaggerated eyes are even better. I have tied a similar pattern with small, medium, and large eyes and fished them under various conditions. The fly with the largest eyes will almost always draw the most strikes.

There are many ways to put eyes on a fly. One of the most common is to paint an eye on the coated thread at the head. The disadvantage of such an eye is that it is so small that it is often not noticed. Sometimes you want to fish a fly with very large eyes, but you want to keep the weight down, so the fly can cast easily and won't sink too deep. There is a practical, easy method of placing tiny to very large eyes that are virtually weightless on a fly. Almost all fly shops stock eyes of various sizes and colors that are printed on lightweight Mylar tape. The tape has an adhesive on the back to press them onto the fly. These eyes range in sizes from ⅛ inch to those of more than a ½ inch in diameter. Because the eyes are printed on brilliant Mylar in highly contrasting colors, they really stand out. It's a good idea to coat the eye once it is positioned on the fly. Flexament, head cement, or clear 5-minute epoxy ensure the eye will stay in place.

Another eye that has gained much popularity the past few years is the lead eye, which is shaped like a dumb bell.

Lead eyes are available in six sizes. Listed here are the weights with the diameter in inches in parentheses: ¹⁄₁₀₀ oz. (⁴⁄₃₂"); ¹⁄₅₀ oz. (⁵⁄₃₂"); ¹⁄₃₆ oz. (³⁄₁₆"); ¹⁄₂₄ oz. (⁷⁄₃₂"); ¹⁄₁₈ oz. (¼"); and ¹⁄₁₀ oz. (⁹⁄₃₂"). For bonefish, I prefer the ¹⁄₅₀- or ¹⁄₁₀₀-ounce lead eyes most of the time. For permit, and when fishing bonefish in water more than 2 feet deep, I use the ¹⁄₂₄-ounce lead eyes. When I am fishing inshore for striped bass, seatrout, snook, and redfish, I use the ¹⁄₂₄-ounce lead eyes. The ¹⁄₁₈- and ¹⁄₁₀-ounce are heavy and require the use of a 9-weight or heavier rod. These two heaviest manufactured lead eyes are superb when you want to drive a fly deep into channels or when fishing a reef. They are also effective when you are offshore and you need to get the fly down quickly, before the fish leave the area.

Some fishermen are now using brass eyes or other metallic eyes instead of those of lead. Brass and antimony eyes weigh about 75 percent of a lead eye of the same volume. The other metallic eyes will not sink as quickly, but that isn't necessarily a liability, because their eyes can be larger. In shallow-water fishing, metallic eyes are often better than lead eyes.

Bead-chain eyes are used on many flies. It was the first attempt to position eyes that carried weight on flies. Bead-chain eyes don't sink a fly as quickly as lead or brass eyes, but they allow you to attach large eyes that are really not very heavy. Bead chain is manufactured in four sizes: #3 is ³⁄₃₂ inch, #6 is ⅛ inch, #10 is ³⁄₁₆ inch, and #13 is ¼ inch. Bead chain is available with a brass, silver, or stainless steel finish.

Another advantage metallic eyes have is that they create additional sound waves in the water when you retrieve them. When waters are dirty from mud or silt, or when the light level is low, large eyes may draw more strikes. The large, protruding eyes create sound waves during the retrieve that radiate out from the head, which alerts nearby fish. This is a major advantage of bead-chain eyes. You can use a very large bead chain, which creates a considerable amount of sound, yet the fly will not sink too rapidly in the water.

Of course, the major reason for using lead, brass, or bead-chain eyes is to force the fly to sink faster. And the faster the fly needs to sink, the heavier the eyes should be. Lead eyes are the best choice for this. The Clouser Minnow works so well because it dives quickly, which allows you to fish deeper in the water column. Flies with weighted eyes also affect the motion of a fly as it is retrieved. If the eyes are located near the head of the pattern, the heavy eyes will cause the fly to dip downward each time the retrieve is stopped. This gives an up-and-down motion to the fly, much like a lead-head jig used on spinning tackle.

Fly Selection and Variations

I believe that almost all fly fishermen are familiar with the Woolly Bugger, one of the deadliest flies in fresh water (and darned good in many saltwater situations, too). Think about it. How many ways can you tie a Woolly Bugger? The original was an unweighted fly, tied with a marabou tail, a chenille body (the body was almost all black or brown), over which was spiraled a hackle—usually grizzly or black color. But now, Woolly Buggers are tied with a host of body materials and colors, and the hackle can be marabou or other materials. Flash material has been added to the body and tail. There are Lead-eye Woollies; Conehead Woollies; and Woolly Buggers with bead heads of glass, brass, lead, or titanium. A Woolly Bugger can be tied on a size 12 or a big size 2/0 hook, which vastly alters its length and bulk.

The point I am making is when you tie Woolly Buggers, you are following the general rules for how the pattern was designed. But you are altering length, color, weight, and much more. That is what you must remember when using the basic list of saltwater flies I am going to suggest.

You can fish successfully in most saltwater situations with six basic flies. They are the Popping Bug, the Surf Candy, the Crab Fly, Lefty's Deceiver, the Clouser Minnow, and the Bendback.

If you are new to saltwater fly fishing, you may know some of these patterns by a host of other names, because many people have slightly altered an original pattern and renamed it. But most fishermen are familiar with the original patterns, and you should have no problem finding out where to buy these flies or how to tie them.

Popping Bug

Poppers are designed to create a disturbance on the surface of the water so that they attract gamefish and create the impression that there is large prey in the vicinity. They can be made from a host of materials, but cork, balsa wood, and closed-cell foam are the most popular. Several design factors can make a Popping Bug easier to cast and more effective as a fly. The hook should be located at the base of the bug, so that it doesn't dive on a backcast. This allows it to pop better, too. Many Popping Bugs have a cupped face, but I believe that if the hook is positioned at the base of the body and the face is slanted forward, the bug will make plenty of noise, and that it will lift from the water easier. Fluffy tails with protruding material drastically increase air resistance, which makes casting difficult. The best bugs have sleek tails so that they don't foul when you cast them.

You will need at least two sizes of poppers. The smaller one should have a face diameter of about ½ inch. The body can be from ¾ inch to 1¼ inches in length. A long shank aids in hookups on any Popping Bug. The tail should be attached so it doesn't tangle on the cast. This is a workhorse bug that you will use for snook, barramundi, bluefish, dolphin, striped bass, or almost any saltwater species that will take a fly. You will need the larger Popping Bug only occasionally, when you need to interest

A collection of Popping Bugs of various colors and sizes.

fish that want a big offering. For example, cobia will often refuse a huge streamer fly but will bust a big noisy bug. A bug with a face about ¾ inch in diameter is sufficient to make all the noise that is required. I do not believe color is important to the fish, but I prefer bright-colored bugs because I can see them better.

Surf Candy

Bob Popovics, perhaps the most innovative fly tier in the world today, developed the Surf Candy, which is a durable fly that performs best when used as an imitation of a small sleek baitfish. The original Surf Candy's forward body was coated in epoxy, but Bob determined later that flexible silicone, such as bathroom tub sealer, gave the fly more action. It's also softer, so when a fish strikes, it is more likely to hang on.

The variations for this pattern are almost limitless, and many imitators have put their name on this pattern. You can build the wing with bucktail or translucent synthetic material. By matching the color of the local baitfish, it is one of the finest flies you can use in salt water.

Crab

I have found crabs in salt water everywhere in the world. Crabs represent a lot of food to predators, and for some species, such as permit, there is no better bait. I recall once fishing with Del Brown, who has caught more than 400 permit on Crab Flies. We found permit sitting just under the surface, obviously rising and taking

Surf Candies

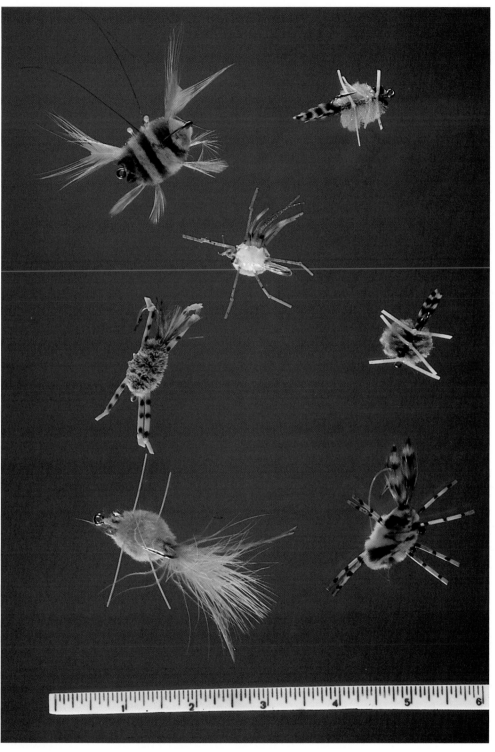

Crab Flies

Tarpon will take Crab Flies.

something close to the top. Del drifted several crab patterns past feeding permit, and they ignored them. But 50-pound tarpon lying below and behind the permit rose eagerly to the flies. Because there was no shock tippet on his line, they quickly broke the leader. Oddly enough, most predatory fish will take crabs large and small, so fish with patterns you can cast easily.

Crab patterns should range from ½ inch to as large as 1½ inches wide. You should have a selection of crabs that float, some that barely sink, and others that are heavily weighted to sink fast. In New England, tiny crabs often hatch in prodigious numbers during late spring on a high tide. A floating Crab Fly the size of a dime fished drag free in the current like a dry fly can be rewarding. For permit, tarpon, and even large stripers, a crab the size of a quarter is really the biggest you need.

One of the important factors for a crab pattern is that the weight must be concentrated at one end of the fly, usually near the eye. The reason for this is apparent when you realize how a crab flees from a predator: It dives at an angle, and so should your pattern.

Bendback

The Bendback fly was developed in the later part of the nineteenth century for bass fishing in the vegetation-cluttered lakes of the South. It is virtually weedless if

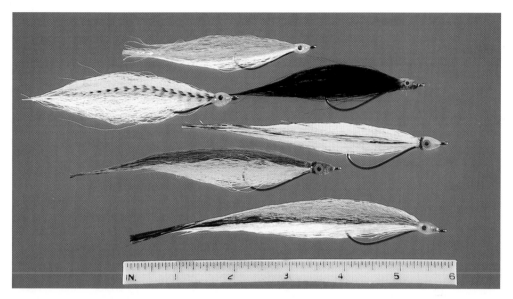

Bendbacks

tied correctly and fished properly, and it has produced better for me than any other weedless fly. I prefer Bendbacks that have no body material on the hook shank, because they swim better, they are easier to cast, and the body material often erodes if it is dragged on the bottom. If I want to fish the fly deep, such as over an oyster bar, I wrap lead wire around the shank just in front of the bend and coat it with epoxy to prevent the wire from detaching. When properly constructed, the wing hides all or most of the hook, and the fly swims with the point up. If you throw the fly into the trees along the water or up on a shoreline, you can gently tease the fly until it travels down the branches or along the shore and drops into the water. It can be fished in the densest weeds without snagging. It is my favorite fly for night fishing at pilings and boat docks, which have many ropes, wires, nails, and other snags. By placing a conehead at the front, this fly can be fished deep with little fear of snagging.

Some of the best Bendbacks are tied to represent baitfish. But attractor patterns can also be tied. One of the best is a bright yellow or white underwing, some flash, and a chartreuse top wing.

Clouser Minnow

This is perhaps the best underwater fly developed in the past 30 years. The Clouser is a favorite of fly fishermen throughout the world for both fresh- and saltwater fishing. As of this writing, I have caught eighty-six species of fish with it. The Clouser has consistently been one of the best flies for redfish, but it is also good for albacore, striped bass, bonito, snook, ladyfish, barramundi, threadfin salmon, dolphin, bluefish, jack crevalle—you name it.

Clousers and Half & Halfs

This permit was taken with a Clouser Minnow.

The Clouser can be tied sparsely, dressed with bulk, made to sink fast or slow depending on the weighted eyes used, and can be made in lengths from 1 inch to 12 inches. Perhaps more than a third of the species I have taken were hooked on a fly with a white or yellow underwing and a chartreuse upperwing. Some professional guides say that "If it ain't chartreuse, it ain't no use." If you use Clousers, be sure to carry a few in this color. In clear water, Clousers tied with translucent synthetics seem to outperform Clousers tied with less translucent materials, such as bucktail. Clousers are often more effective if several different colors of flash material are integrated into the wing.

Lefty's Deceiver

The Clouser Minnow and the Lefty's Deceiver are perhaps the two most frequently used saltwater flies around the world. The Lefty's Deceiver been used for decades to catch everything from billfish to small estuary species. As with the Woolly Bugger and the other flies I've described, you can change the size and color combinations, add or delete weight, make it long or short, and use flash material in the wing or use no flash material at all. A host of imitators have placed their name on the fly, but the basic fly remains the same.

Lefty's Deceivers

Tied sparsely, Lefty's Deceiver imitates a sleek baitfish, such as a sand eel, or it can have lead wire on the shank and be tied bulky, such as the well-known Grocery Fly used in New England. One of the best variations over the years is all black with a red throat of Mylar and some purple Mylar flash on the sides.

To summarize: You will be able to fish successfully in most saltwater situations by using these six flies if you keep in mind the suggested guidelines. There will be occasions when a different pattern will outfish them, but you will always be well prepared if you carry these.

Bonefish

The one species exception to the above-listed patterns is the bonefish. Scientists have proven that bonefish will eat almost anything they can catch and get down their throats. That means that a host of flies are effective, but you only need a very few patterns to successfully fish for bones. If you carry a lot of others, they will probably work, too.

Most of the time you should match the color of the bottom with your fly. On dark turtle grass, a darker fly is advisable. Conversely, on a light bottom, choose a lighter fly. Another thing to note is that when seeking tiny bonefish, from ½ pound to 3 pounds, I would suggest using a size 4 fly, with a few size 6s for very calm condi-

A basic bonefish fly selection.

tions. For bonefish larger than 3 pounds, I rarely use a fly smaller than size 4. If the bonefish are averaging 4 pounds or larger, my best success has been with size 2 hooks.

Here are the five bonefish patterns that will serve you well in most of the world. Some of them are repeated from the list above, but the additional details are specific to bonefish.

Clouser Minnow

If I had to fish with only two bonefish flies, I would choose these two Clouser Minnows. Both are tied the same way, with a white bucktail underwing and pearl flash material in the middle. The upperwing should use either chartreuse bucktail or light tan bucktail, about the color of khaki pants. If you're fishing for very large bonefish, the fly should be about 2½ to 3 inches long.

Gotcha

Next to the two Clousers, the Gotcha is the hottest fly I have ever used on light-colored bonefish flats. It is essentially a Crazy Charlie with an extended pink nose, which seems to be a trigger for bonefish. I am never without a few of these.

Tailing Bendback

This fly is essential because bonefish will frequently go into water so shallow that their backs may actually be above the surface. The two requirements for fishing a Tailing Bendback in these conditions are that the fly must land with a minimum of noise, and it must be fished over a rocky bottom. I recommend a fly that has no body material and a rather full wing. This results in a silent splash down and causes the fly to ride just below the surface.

Snapping Shrimp

This pattern is reliable when fished where the bottom is dark. I often tie the pattern as a Bendback if I will be fishing in dense turtle grass so it can slither through the vegetation. It resembles a brownish snapping shrimp with an orange claw. It is my favorite for a dark bottom.

Crab Fly

My bonefish box always has a few Crab Flies in it. They can be made from a host of materials. The most effective patterns are usually made from a soft material, such as rug yarn, trimmed sheep's wool, or Furry Foam. The Crab Fly is also a superior pattern for permit, which are often found on the same flats as bones. If the bot-

This basic saltwater fly selection will catch fish nearly anywhere.

tom is very light in color, a cream-colored crab often produces well. For most situations, a crab that is dark—usually a greenish color—is often preferred. The bonefish Crab Fly should be lightly weighted; metallic eyes are often used to do this. The best results are usually obtained if the weight is concentrated on one end.

With the six basic flies and the five bonefish flies, you have all the flies you need to start fly fishing in salt water. The next step is to improve your presentation, which, after all, is the key to catching most fish on a fly.

II. FISHING

C H A P T E R 6

Casting

asting is a stumbling block in the transition from fly fishing in fresh water to fly fishing in salt water. Almost any saltwater guide will tell you the biggest difficulty for most freshwater anglers is that they simply can't cast well enough to take advantage of ordinary saltwater fishing situations. The three reasons for this are larger flies, wind, and distance. A size-4 long-shank hook with a little weight attached is considered to be a heavy fly when fly fishing for trout, and the average casting distance is probably 15 to 35 feet. That's where you *start* in salt water!

Many newcomers to saltwater fly fishing wonder about the emphasis on distance. In most freshwater situations, anglers who can cast to 45 or 50 feet can handle just about any casting chore that confronts them. In the salt, many things are different. The ability to throw a longer line is not only desirable—it's vital to success.

In fresh water, the angler can often move around, get into position, and cast. More often than not, in salt water you have to make the cast from wherever you happen to be, and it may not be the best position. You may also have to cast into the wind. There are very few wind-free days when saltwater fly fishing, and you don't get to cast downwind very often. When stalking a fish on the flats, it may be moving a bit faster than the guide or friend can pole the boat, which often means that you aren't going to get a shot unless you can make a long cast. Anyone who has poled a boat after a shark has learned that while the shark seems to be meandering slowly across the shallows, it's moving surprisingly fast.

make another. That means you must bring the hands together, so you can make another pull. Unless this is done with great care, slack forms between the two hands that must be removed before you can begin the forward cast. Third, the size of the loop is determined by the distance the rod tip speeds up and stops at the very end of the cast. Long hauls will cause the rod to flex deeper and form larger loops. Fourth, and most important, the line speed is determined to a great extent by how quickly the rod stops at the end of the cast. If you follow through with the rod tip, you diminish line speed. If the rod hand makes a nice, short speed-up-and-stop, but the line hand continues to pull on the rod tip, the tip doesn't stop. This causes a considerable loss of energy in the cast.

So how do you make a good double haul? First, consider what the rod does during a cast. It gradually accelerates until the final moment of the cast, when the rod is drastically accelerated to make a speed-up-and-stop. The length of the speed-up-and-stop determines the loop size. If you want to make the most efficient haul, obtain the greatest amount of line speed, and have a tight loop, you must mirror the action of the rod. In other words, the way the rod loads and forms the speed-up-and-stop should be duplicated with the haul.

Throughout the double haul, keep the line hand close to the casting hand. At this stage of the backcast, the haul should be accelerated simultaneously with the speed of the rod.

At the moment the rod speeds up and stops, the haul likewise accelerates and stops. Note the distance between the line hand and the casting hand: To haul effectively you must haul quicker, not longer.

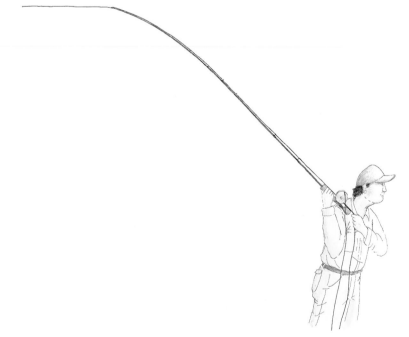

During the time that it takes for the line to unroll behind you, reposition the line hand close to the casting hand in preparation for the forward haul.

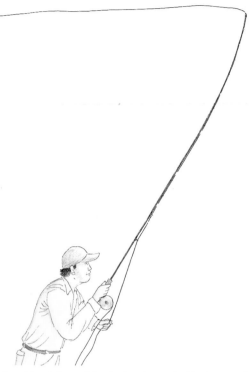

The moment before the speed-up-and-stop, the haul is at its quickest. Again, note that even at the peak speed of the haul, the line hand is relatively close to the casting hand.

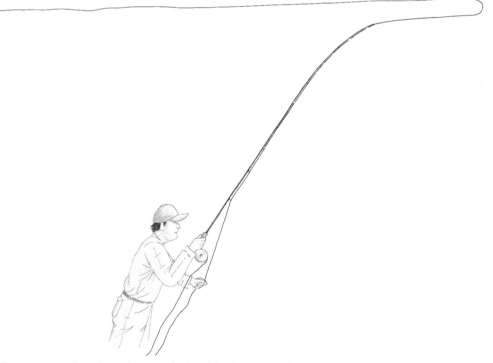

The moment when the rod stops, the haul is also stopped.

There are two segments of rod movement on any cast. There is a gradual acceleration of the rod, which culminates in an extremely short, fast speed-up-and-stop. This is what you want to do with the haul. During the time the rod is being swept forward at an increasing speed, the haul should also be increasing in speed. That is the first of the two parts of a haul. The second part of the haul is performed during the second part of the rod stroke. The rod hand and the haul hand are accelerated simultaneously during the speed-up-and-stop. The haul should mirror the rod's action throughout the cast.

The Extra-Effort Cast

It's an old story to anyone experienced in fly fishing the salt. You want to make longer cast, and when you do, you usually spoil the cast. The angler makes two nicely controlled false casts. Then, with a furious haul on the line and with tremendous force in the rod hand, an attempt is made to throw the fly into the next zip code, but the cast completely falls apart. Why does this happen, and how can we eliminate the problem and make that extra-effort cast?

If the angler knows how to double haul correctly, the mission can be accomplished. Make two false casts with as much line extended from the tip as you can comfortably handle. On the final cast, make an identical false cast. This means the loop will be nicely controlled, and there will be no shock waves in the line. But, make the double haul (as suggested earlier) much faster. Don't make a longer haul on the forward cast, just make a faster haul.

Here's what happens. The only way to make your line go faster is by making the rod tip speed up faster and stop quicker. The faster the haul, the greater it accelerates the rod tip. To obtain distance, you simply increase tip speed with a faster haul. *But because you did not alter the false cast,* you will maintain a good loop, and distance will follow.

There is an important casting message here. Whenever you need to make an extra-effort cast of any kind, the extra help should come from the line hand and a faster haul. Invariably, what happens is that the angler tries to get the effort out of the rod hand, which destroys the loop. Let me give you another example that you can demonstrate to yourself. Lay out more line on the water than you can comfortably pick up. Make a backcast, attempting to accomplish most of it with the rod hand—as most anglers do. The cast can be made, but with difficulty. Now make a nice controlled backcast with the rod hand, but during the speed-up-and-stop portion, greatly accelerate the line hand during the haul. You may be surprised how much line you can now pick up. The message, again, is that when you need to make an extra-effort cast, use a faster haul.

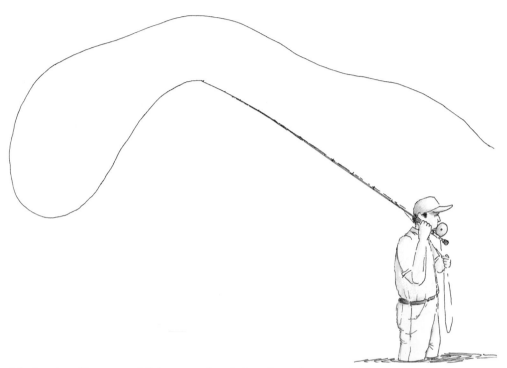

Most extra-effort casts fail because they bring the rod up vertically on the backcast. This forces the rod tip down at the end of the backcast and causes a loose sag in the fly line that must be eliminated before an effective forward cast is made. If there is any slack between the line hand and the end of the fly line, it makes matters worse.

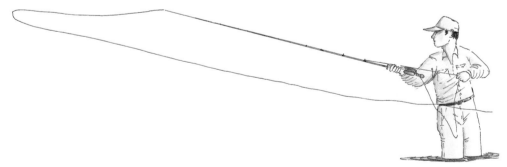

Make sure that there is no slack between the line hand and the end of the fly line before the backcast. Touch the rod tip to the water and make a sidearm backcast. The trajectory should follow a wedge shape. Make sure that the rod tip doesn't get higher than your head until it is behind you, or the line will sag as in the previous illustration. When you have stopped the rod in an upward direction, you can make an effective forward cast.

The Roll Cast

The roll cast is the most frequently used cast in fly fishing after the basic forward cast. Fishermen use it when they have no room to backcast or when they are working with deep-sinking lines. The roll cast is often effective in dislodging a fly that is stuck in a distant log or branch. By making a roll cast, allowing the leader to travel beyond the log, and then making a quick backcast, you can generally dislodge the fly. The roll cast can also be used to remove vegetation on a hook while you are retrieving. Retrieve the fly close enough to make an easy roll cast. Then make a gentle roll cast that is directed toward the fly. When all of the line is in the air, but the fly is still underwater, make a violent backcast. The water will cling to the vegetation, and if the backcast is made with extra speed, the hook should shear through the vegetation, which saves you the hassle of handling the hook to free it of the grass. There are many other situations in which this cast will aid the angler in getting a better presentation. But many, if not most, fly fishermen who perform the roll cast watch as the leader and forward end of their line crashes short of the target in a tangled mess.

The correct efficient roll cast is extremely easy to master. I believe the reason why most fly fishermen have trouble with the roll cast is that for decades, books, casting instructors, and even modern videos have been teaching the same inefficient system developed decades ago.

To perform a better roll cast, the angler must realize that the line and fly will go in the direction that you stop the rod tip at the end of the cast, and that the longer the rod moves during the cast, the more power you can put into the cast. If you understand these two things, you will immediately improve your roll cast.

If you look at most books and videos, they teach that you raise the elbow and elevate the rod tip to a vertical position tilted slightly behind you. It is then suggested that the rod be swept forward and down. Three detrimental things occur when this happens. First, the rod travels through a very short arc, which means it will offer little help in delivering the cast. Second, the size of a loop during any cast is determined by the distance the rod tip moves during the power stroke at the end of the cast. If the rod is swept from the original elevated position and stops just above the surface, then the rod is being asked to throw the line around a wide arc—instead of delivering the energy of the cast toward the target. Third, the line is going to go in the direction in which you stop the rod tip at the end of the cast, which is down in front of you. This is why most roll casts end a short distance from the angler and with the forward portion in a tangled pile. Fortunately, you only have to do a few simple things to make a good roll cast.

If you want to improve your roll cast, you should understand that you are only going to modify the backcast. You still want to make a normal forward cast.

It is important that your elbow be held at its normal height throughout the cast. If the elbow rises or falls on the forward stroke, the line will also rise or fall, instead of traveling toward the target. Draw the rod and line back slowly. The longer the roll cast, the farther back the rod should be. Ideally, if the fishing situation allows, the best and easiest roll cast can be made when the rod is positioned behind the angler and parallel with the water. Allow the front end of the line to stop. It need only pause a heartbeat. That is long enough for surface tension to grip the fly line. You need the water's tension to grip the rod so that it can have something to pull against and load for the forward cast. If you don't let the line end stop, it is very difficult to make a good roll cast.

You are now ready to make the roll cast. You have modified your backcast—but don't modify your forward cast. Make a normal forward cast, directed about eye level. Bring the hand forward at the same height, keeping the elbow parallel to the water during the forward cast. Now all of the energy in the cast is directed toward the target. If you need to make a longer roll cast, you can increase the tip speed and stop quicker, or you can make a haul with your line hand, but only on the forward cast.

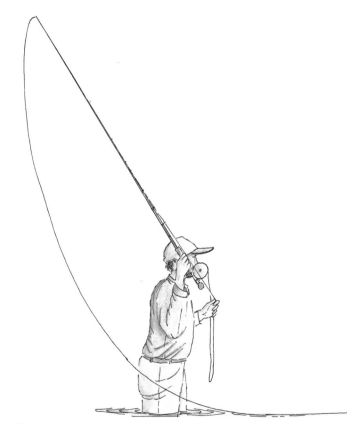

Ineffective roll casts start with the rod tip high.

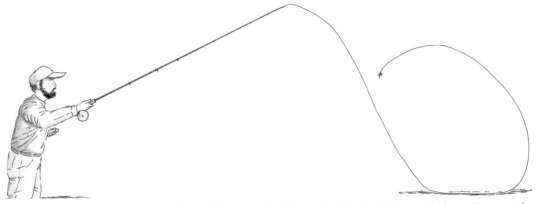

When you start with the rod tip high, the energy in the cast is directed into a wide loop. Because the line will travel in the direction in which the rod tip speeds up and stops, the end of the loop will be in front of you, and the line will pile up there with a splash.

Effective roll casts start with the rod tip as far back as you can get it. The height of your elbow should be at its height at rest, and your casting hand should be below your shoulder. Before the forward cast, let the line come to a complete stop. This lets you use the surface tension of the water to load the line on the forward cast. Make a normal sidearm forward cast.

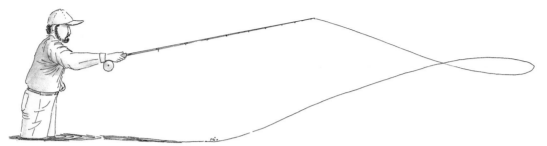

On the forward cast, imagine that the water you are casting to is at eye level. If your rod hand travels straight ahead, the line will go straight ahead, as shown here. If your rod hand rises, the loop will get larger. If the rod tip stops in the direction of the water, the line will pile up.

Weighted Lines

Floating lines are popular for working shallows and flats. Most fishermen agree that casting weighted lines—such as the Teeny series, lead-core shooting heads, and similar lines—is a frustrating and disagreeable task. The fear of getting hit with the line or fly, the chance of breaking a rod from the fly's impact, and the extra effort involved in casting has also caused many fly fishermen to avoid these useful lines. Instead, fly fishermen continue to use a floating line when they know they would do far better with a sinking type. Yet when you learn how to properly throw a weighted line, it is the easiest of all lines to cast.

With a floating line, not only is it difficult to get a fly more than 5 or 6 feet deep, but to cast a big fly or heavily weighted fly, you'll need an 11- or 12-weight floating line. The large, wind-resistant diameter of this buoyant line makes it extremely difficult to throw, especially into a breeze. But if you cast a thin, similarly weighted line with the same fly, the chore becomes far less difficult. No line will cast into the wind like the lead core, the well-known Teeny line, or similarly constructed lines, which have a thin, floating running line and a fast-sinking belly. Because of their mass and thin diameter, they cut through the wind better than all other fly lines.

Another occasion for using sinking lines is when you are fly fishing from the beach. A floating line bobs up and down on rough surf, which alters your retrieve. It can spoil the action you are trying to impart to the fly and create unwanted slack that may cause a missed strike. Worse, the floating line remains on top as it is retrieved, and your fly doesn't get down near the bottom, where the fish are.

There many other reasons for using sinking lines and flies. Freshwater trout take most of their food beneath the surface, and so do most saltwater fish. Florida, the Bahamas, Christmas Island, and other exotic destinations offer shallow-water flats fishing, but most fly fishermen seek their quarry near home. Local waters are often deep, or there may be channels that need to be explored. Whether you are fishing for kelp bass in California, salmon off Oregon and Washington, bluefish near the Outer Banks of North Carolina, or stripers off Montauk, you frequently need to get the fly well below the surface.

With some species, especially striped bass, the largest fish are almost always concentrated below the smaller ones in a school. When the fish are breaking—or rounding baitfish up to the surface in a concentrated feeding frenzy—experienced striper fishermen will use a fast sinking line and a weighted fly instead of trying to catch the fish on the surface. They cast into the melee and allow the line and fly to sink well below all the frantic surface action. When they begin their retrieve, they are often rewarded with far larger fish. This also works with bluefish. When they are breaking on the surface, the big seatrout stay well below them and feed on the chopped bait that the bluefish destroyed.

Casting Weighted Lines and Flies

Once you understand the problems that weighted lines and flies present, you can make adjustments to your casting, and they'll become a joy to throw. One problem is that fishermen cast a weighted line or fly the same way they do a floating line. When they do this, the backcast causes the problem. Floating lines tend to slow down near the end of the backcast. That is why instructors teach fly fishermen to accelerate rapidly with the rod tip to develop enough speed to keep a floating line traveling fast throughout the backcast.

When you backcast a weighted line as you would a floating line, once the weighted line and/or fly is moving at a high speed, its inertia tends to keep it moving. When the forward cast is made, the heavy line and fly, which are traveling *away* from the target, have to suddenly make a 180-degree turn and go the other way. This quick change in direction causes the problem.

With a floating line, you want a fast backcast to maintain a tight loop. What you want to do with a weighted line on the backcast is just the opposite. You want to make a backcast that goes back slowly, with just enough speed to complete the cast, and a wide loop. This permits the line to travel slowly back and round a curve, so that the change in direction from the backcast to the forward cast isn't abrupt.

To accomplish this, the line must be lifted to the surface before the backcast can be made. If you are fishing a weighted fly, a lead-core line, a sinking shooting head line, or a Teeny line that has more than 20 feet of the forward section that is weighted, you need to retrieve until the rear of the sinking portion is at the rod tip. The thin shooting line is not stiff enough to lift this heavy line. Once you have the correct amount of line retrieved, make a roll cast. If the roll cast did not lay out in front of you, make another roll cast. Never make a false cast with sinking lines or

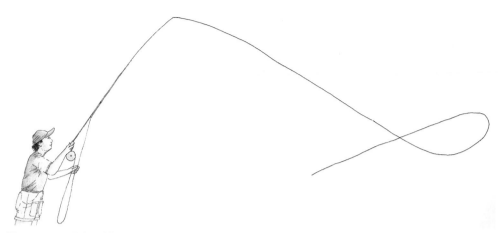

To cast a weighted line, start with a roll cast. This will lift the line toward the surface of the water. If the line is not on the surface of the water before your backcast, make another roll cast.

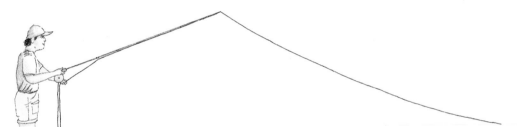

When the line is laid out straight and on the surface, begin the backcast. Be sure to make the backcast before the line begins to sink.

When making the backcast with a weighted line, make a wide sidearm loop. Note that the elbow should stay at its normal resting height or the loop may be too wide on the forward cast.

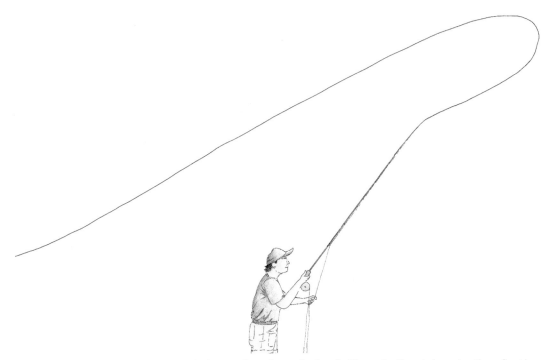

For the forward cast, make a gentle forward stroke and a haul. Since the line is heavier than floating line, you must cast the line in an upward trajectory to get more distance.

heavy flies—it causes a quick change of direction in the cast. Although it is possible to do so, timing is much more critical and difficult. Instead, always make a roll cast so that you can make a good backcast. At the end of the roll cast, watch the line end. When it unrolls, or straightens on the water, it is time for step two. You can't wait too long, or the line will sink too far below the surface and you will need to make another roll cast. But if you begin the backcast as soon as the front end of the line strikes the water, even with a lead-core shooting head, it will remain close to the surface. Keeping the rod tip low (as if you were making a low side cast), slowly draw the line and rod back. Be sure to keep your elbow hanging at its normal height. If you raise the elbow, you will adversely affect the forward cast. When the rod is pointed about 45 degrees in front of you as you are drawing back the line, start to make a wide-loop backcast by pulling the rod tip continuously around a curve. I explain to casters that it is like pulling the rod tip inside a horseshoe. You must pull all the way around the horseshoe. This will cause the line to make the wide loop of a horseshoe and gradually change the direction of the line from a backcast to a forward cast.

Again, it is important that your elbow stay at its normal level throughout the cast. If it doesn't, there is a good chance that you will pull the loop too wide on the forward cast. Once the backcast is ended, make a normal forward cast. Two important factors are involved in making forward casts with sinking lines. The first is that you should use a gentle forward stroke and haul. Too much force will cause unwanted shock waves, wide loops, and loss of control. The second is that by angling the cast at a steep climb in front of you, you will obtain more distance.

In summary, never false cast the line. Roll cast to get the line to the surface and slow down the entire backcast. Make sure the backcast goes around a wide curve. Be sure to keep the elbow below the shoulder throughout the cast. And finally, make the forward cast at a steep angle.

If you follow these rules, you'll see that casting sinking lines is much easier than casting floating lines, and you will never be struck by the line or the fly.

The Change-of-Direction Cast

This is one of the easiest and most useful casts to learn. It is not a long-distance cast but is very effective to about 40 feet. There are numerous situations in which

For the change-of-direction cast, face the new target and drag the fly line until the rod tip points at the new target. Do not stop the rod tip, but immediately start the backcast with the rod tip near the surface of the water.

this cast is helpful. If you just made a cast on the platform of a boat at 10 o'clock to a cruising fish, and the person in the back of the boat yells, "Quick, make a cast at 2 o'clock," the change in direction can be made with one backcast. Most people make several backcasts before delivering the fly.

The key to making any good forward cast is to set up a backcast as nearly directly opposite from the target as possible. If you can make the first backcast exactly

Make a backcast in the direction opposite the new target. A haul on the backcast is especially beneficial, because it will help to eliminate slack that is created when you drag the line toward the direction of the new target.

If the backcast is directed opposite the new target, the forward cast should be simple.

away from the target, it will be the only backcast you need to deliver the fly to the target.

The Extra-High Backcast

The fly fisherman often has to contend with an extra-high bank behind him or a background that has a hole in it that would allow her to make a backcast, but only if she can hit the hole with her fly line. When most fishermen try to cast in this situation, they rod in a normal manner, so that the knuckles of their hand face the target and restrict how high they can make a backcast. The line will always go in the direction that the rod tip stops. If you hold the rod this way, you can only move so far upward—the rest of the energy will be directed back toward what you want to avoid hitting. Try the motion and you can see what I mean.

The only caution to mention is that this cast works to about 40 feet—longer casts are often difficult. But it can help you get to many fish that would be impossible with the conventional backcast.

When you attempt to make a conventional extra-high backcast, your hand can only reach a certain height.

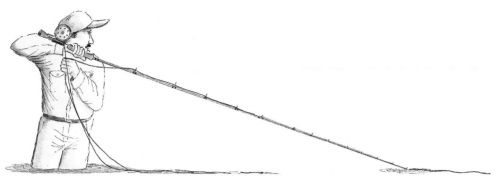

To make a successful extra-high backcast, position your thumb underneath *the rod and begin the backcast with the rod tip just touching the water.*

Because your hand, elbow, and shoulder can extend directly upward, you can accomplish a nearly vertical backcast. As soon as the backcast is made, turn your hand back toward the target and make a normal forward cast.

How to See Fish

The angler must see a fish before making a cast in nearly all saltwater fly-fishing situations. This is especially true if you are fishing the shallows. The sooner the fish can be located, the better, because it allows more time to decide where to throw the fly and to finally deliver it. Fortunately, there are easily mastered techniques to help the angler.

Perhaps the first thing to realize is that you may not be looking for something that looks like a fish. Many fish—such as stripers, permit, tarpon, and bonefish—have silver sides, which act just like a mirror to reflect the environment or bottom over which they are swimming. A very large striper could be swimming in 3 feet of water and be almost invisible.

So the first thing to learn about looking for fish is not to expect to see an entire fish. The top of the back and part of the tail fin of a permit has a slightly darker coloration. When you see a thin black line knifing through the water, it may indicate the presence of a 30-pound or larger fish. Bonefish are very difficult to see. You should look for the large eye, the slightly pale green or blue color of the tail, or the slightly darker shading of the back. From the side, the striped bass is nearly invisible, because the silvery side is in effect a mirror. What gives it away is the slighter darker green back.

To see well, you need the proper tools, which are fortunately few in number. If you fish and don't wear a hat, you are at a distinct disadvantage. You need a hat to

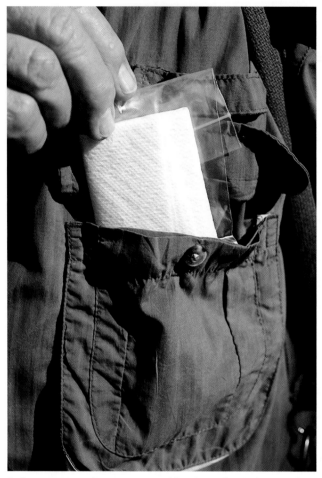

I always carry clean paper napkins in a plastic bag to clean my polarized sunglasses.

shade the eyes to see well. The color of the underside of the brim is very important. It should be black in color, or very dark. Hats with a light underbrim reflect the light bouncing off the water into the eyes, which reduces your chances of seeing well.

Polarized glasses are important, too. I favor different colors for different conditions. For most fishing, the brown/yellow colored glasses are best. On overcast or rainy days, I wear bright yellow glasses, and for offshore fishing, blue-gray glasses seem to let sight penetrate the water better.

Whatever kind of polarized glasses you wear, be sure to have side shields on the frames. These prevent glare from the water at your side or behind you. It is advisable to carry some glass cleaner to remove salt spray. I carry paper napkins in a small plastic bag that are dry and can be used to keep my glasses clean.

If you tilt your head to the left or to the right, you can remove additional glare. Try this from time to time as you search for fish.

Finding Fish in the Flats

The time of the year often influences how well you can see fish in the shallows. The best light is when there is a cloud-free sky and the sun is high overhead. The lower the angle of the sun, the more difficult it is to see into the water. One reason Christmas Island is so ideal for bonefishing is because it is located on the equator. For most of the day, the sun is high above the horizon. Fishermen who travel to Florida or the Bahamas during the winter may be disappointed because they are rather far from the equator. The sun doesn't get high enough until about 9 A.M., and by 4 P.M. spotting fish becomes difficult again. But in the summer months, you could fish 2 or 3 hours earlier and later, simply because the angle of the sun is higher.

If you are fishing from a boat, try not to stare at the water—you'll see little. Scan the area constantly and not just the waters in front of you. Examine the water as far away as you can locate fish. Look for bonefish to a distance of at least 50 yards. Tarpon often roll and break the surface, and you can see them as far away as 200 yards.

When wading the shallows, try to look as far ahead as possible to see fish. As you move along, try to keep the sun at your back or side. If you look into the sun's glare, many fish will escape your notice. You can often improve your chances on days when the light is low or overcast. Try fishing along a shoreline with dark foliage, where the fish will be detected more easily. You can also see them better if there is a storm in the background. Poling toward a bright cloud on the horizon can ruin your ability to see well. But poling toward a dark cloud improves your ability to locate fish. Another good time to fish shorelines is when they are leeward when the wind is blowing, because calm water aids greatly in seeing fish.

One of the most important tricks for seeing fish is to understand that when fish are in less than a foot of water, they will make a wake. This disturbance is easy to see. But remember when you make your cast that the fish will be in front of the wake.

The conditions are nearly perfect for this angler: There are clouds on the horizon and dark foliage to reduce glare. He should be able to see the fish quite clearly.

When bonefish swim in the shallows, their tails often come out of the water.

Be sure to cast well ahead of a fish when it produces a wake.

If you see tiny ripples in a calm area—this is called nervous water—it is an indicator that fish are swimming under those little ripples. Also, be aware of wave patterns. If the waves are coming from one direction, and one wave is not following the same pattern, it may be caused by swimming fish.

Varied colors on a shallow flat can also be a good place for fish. Snook, seatrout, barracuda, and other species enjoy lying in white sand holes on a flat, so check them carefully. Dark spots can also be a good place to search. Logs, coral heads, and other debris on a flat are often ambush spots or hideouts for many species.

Look for muddy places, too. Some fish, such as bonefish, will try to root out crabs, shrimp, and other foods from the bottom. This will cause small but visible puffs of mud. Various types of rays can also be helpful. They will cruise along, then drop to the bottom and pound their wings to flush out food there. Because the rays swim slowly, many fast gamefish take advantage of this. They will hover close to a ray, and when shrimp, crabs, and other morsels try to flee the ray, the faster-moving fish grab them before the ray can. Even when rays are not pounding the bottom, many predatory fish will swim alongside them. So anytime you see a ray pounding the bottom or swimming, check it out.

When gamefish chase a school of baitfish to the surface, the water becomes alive. Casting just off this "nervous water" is almost sure to catch fish.

The dark spots against the sandy background are bonefish.

Night Fishing

At night, docks and bridges with lights attract small bait and shrimp. These foods in turn draw predatory fish. Learning to see these fish is easy and can produce some excellent fishing. The predatory fish will always be holding on the uptide side of such a lighted area. For example, if the tide is flowing from north to south, the fish will be on the north side. To locate the fish, examine where the shadow line falls on the water. The fish will be just inside that shadow line, facing into the current. They will appear as a dark shadow. Once you know what you are looking for, they are easy to see.

Deeper Water and Offshore Fishing

When fish swim in water more than a foot deep, they make no wake, unless they are very large. Then, you should look at the bottom. This sounds logical, but many fishermen don't do it. Let me give an example of how not looking at the bottom may prevent someone from seeing fish. If you look in a store window at items just inside the window, you don't see anything farther back inside the store. But if you look through the window at the back of the store, anyone moving between you

Bones and other fish like to hang around debris.

Redfish and bonefish will try to disturb shrimp and crab found in the mud. This is called "mudding" and causes puffs of mud to rise to the surface.

Always examine swimming rays. Gamefish often follow them around to steal the food that the rays flush from the bottom.

By concentrating on the sea floor, you can often spot well-concealed fish like this redfish.

and the back of the store will interrupt your vision. By concentrating on the bottom, you will see any fish swimming across it.

Birds that obtain their food from the sea are among the best aids. Any time you see birds diving to the water, you know that baitfish may be pushed to the surface, and gamefish will often be under them. A flock of birds that are just resting on the surface can be a good indicator. The birds may know that a large school of bait is underneath them. They are simply waiting for predatory fish to come along and begin feeding. If you have no place special to go, it may be worth staying nearby.

The frigate bird, a large bird with W-shaped wings, is a good indicator of large fish in the area. These birds frequently follow billfish, tuna, and other large species. If you see a frigate bird lazily gliding overhead, keep a watch on it. And if the bird suddenly dives toward the surface, you can almost be certain that big fish are there.

An oil slick may form on the surface when tuna, mackerel, or bluefish are feeding well below the surface. Many baitfish contain a great deal of oil. When predatory fish chop into them, the oil is released and comes to the surface, which forms a slick.

Always search for white splashes on the horizon, or leaping fish. There are few places in the sea where small fish can hide from predators. Floating debris, such as trees, logs, boards, old boxes, and large patches of grass are where these smaller fish hide. Always check such debris for fish.

Birds feed on baitfish and often reveal where gamefish may be lurking.

One thing you almost never want to do is throw a fly close to a fish, then let it slowly tumble or sink without any action. The only exception would be presenting a Crab Fly to a permit.

In almost all retrieves, you should not use the rod to manipulate the fly. Instead, vary the speed and length of the pulls you make with the line hand to obtain the necessary action. Keep your rod pointed at the fly, with the tip almost in the water. If a fish strikes, the line is free of slack and you can set the hook quickly.

There are a few exceptions to this. When tempting a big jack crevalle with a Popping Bug, or when fishing for king mackerel, sudden long sweeps of the rod can generate a tremendously fast leap through the water with the fly and turn a reluctant fish into one that will smash your offering. But with most other fish, this special technique will simply defeat your purpose.

Whenever possible, watch your fly closely, especially when a fish swims near the fly. Usually, it is easy to watch both when the fish is near. If you can see the fly and the fish's actions, you can determine whether you need to alter the retrieve. One commonly held belief is that you should wait before striking until a tarpon grabs your fly and turns. The problem is that often a tarpon will take the fly and continue straight ahead. If you can see the fly, you can strike when the tarpon closes its mouth.

If you point your rod tip toward the fly, you reduce the slack in the line, which will give you a better chance to detect a strike and react in time.

A Jack Crevalle will hit a fast Popping Bug.

If a fish follows your fly for 6 to 8 feet and doesn't take it, change your retrieve. One good trick is to make two or three quick line pulls to give the appearance that the fly is in trouble and is trying to flee the gamefish. That will usually draw a strike.

When retrieving an underwater fly, you should almost never stop the retrieve or allow the fly to lie motionless. Even if the fly remains in a small area, give it at least a tiny bit of lifelike action. The one instance when this is not true is when presenting a crab pattern to a permit. If the permit seems to be examining the Crab Fly, don't move it. A crab isn't going to dance around on the bottom and give itself away when a permit is looking at it.

When you are fishing for striped bass with Popping Bugs, the reverse is often true. If you give the bug a lot of action during the retrieve, you can frequently induce fish to strike. The amount of noise you make with a Popping Bug should depend on the water conditions. When there is a bit of chop on the water, you should make extra noise. But there are occasions when a noisy retrieve is disastrous. If you are fishing for large fish that are cruising the shallows, a loud Popping Bug can frighten them. A splashy retrieve with a bug will draw a zero in backcountry mangrove coves or creeks, where the water is slick and calm. Instead, start fishing with a very gentle retrieve so that the bug barely disturbs the surface, or use a Slider (a Popping Bug with a bullet-shaped head) that can be retrieved so that it creates a small wake on the surface but makes no audible noise.

One of the most critical factors in retrieving is the sink rate of the fly. If you use a fast-sinking fly on a shallow grass flat, you will be constantly fighting weeds. Species that feed in the water column or near the top, such as striped bass, bluefish, albacore, and tarpon, will rarely take a fly that swims below them. Bottom-feeding species, however, such as bonefish, redfish, and permit, will dive down to take your fly. You must keep the sink rate of the fly in mind, so that it is far enough ahead of any species that feed in the water column, and be sure that the fly descends at the same level as the fish, or slightly above it. This important retrieve factor is often over-looked. When chumming, for example, the chum fly should drift at the same depth as the chum. If the fly drifts well below or above the fish, you reduce your chances of taking fish.

You will need to alter your retrieve a bit for some species, too. My best luck with barracuda, for example, is to cast the fly 4 or 5 feet in front of it. The moment the fly contacts the water, make a backcast. This causes the fly to speed across the surface in front of the 'cuda and disappear. Repeat this cast several times, then drop the fly down and make a fairly rapid retrieve. The 'cuda will often take.

There is another retrieve trick that has just about doubled my hookups on bonefish. As you retrieve, you'll often feel little taps on the line. Many times this is actually a bonefish picking up your fly and discarding it. This occurs between the period when you drop the line while stripping and are moving the hand forward to grip the line again. When I know the fish is within a few feet of the fly, stalking it, I stop the standard erratic retrieve and begin a long, slow pull of the line. This drags the fly very slowly, and consistently, along the bottom. The key here is to pull on the line only enough to keep the fly barely moving on the bottom. This insures that the line and leader remain taut between your hand and the fly. When the bonefish picks up the fly, you are immediately aware of it, and a gentle tug will ensure a hookup. If the bonefish doesn't strike, but follows the fly for the length of this long draw (I carry the line back on the slow draw as far as the hand can reach behind me), I'll make an-other long draw. If that doesn't work, I follow that with a few 18-inch long quick strips, which generally triggers a strike.

Many fly fishermen do not consider the importance of retrieving. If you try these methods, you'll catch more fish.

CHAPTER 9

Inshore
Fly Fishing

Perhaps 95 percent of all saltwater fly fishermen enjoy their sport inshore. Inshore fishing takes place within a few miles of the beaches, usually in boats no longer than 23 feet.

There are two inshore areas that differ greatly, and they should be discussed separately. One is the general inshore, which includes fishing from the beach, from jetties, from small boats, at inlets, in rivers, and over wrecks while chumming. The other area is the backcountry and flats. Flats fishing is done in New England or the Bahamas. Backcountry occurs in the generally shallow waters of estuaries, where there is a mingling of salt and fresh waters. Flats fishing and backcountry fishing will be discussed in Chapter 10.

General Inshore

Several factors affect inshore fly fishing, including tide, temperature, bait, depth, and structure. Gamefish follow baitfish, which are in turn affected by the tide and the seasons. While there are many species of baitfish offshore, the inshore waters are where most of the major schools are to be found—and that's why so many gamefish are caught there. It's their grocery store. A few species are not as mobile, such as fluke. They will remain in one location until the falling temperatures move their food supply.

Much of this fishing is done in waters that range from a few feet to perhaps 30 feet in depth, so you really need at least two types of fly lines. A floating line will do for much of it, but the line that is most valuable and will see the most action is a fast-sinking head, as discussed previously. Remember, you'll have to get that fly down to where the fish are holding.

Structure determines where many fish will be. A submerged wreck furnishes shelter for small fish, which draw the larger fish we seek. Buoys, channel markers, and towers that rise above the surface all attract baitfish. Structure can also be a sudden descent (drop-off) of the sea floor. That's why it's so important to have a depth finder if you fish waters where you can't physically see the bottom. Other hot spots include points of land that project out into the water, especially if the point drops off quickly or if it has an underwater structure. Anywhere a river enters inshore waters can be a potentially good place to cast. Floating vegetation or debris flows down the river and furnishes hiding places for baitfish, so these are areas for the fly fisherman to investigate.

Fish congregate near the tips of small peninsulas.

Approaching Breaking Fish

Predator fish force bait to the surface, where they can capture it. When this happens, the surface is broken by the splashes of fish jumping out of the water—we call this *breaking fish*. If you can get to these fish while they are feeding frantically, you have a good chance of getting them to accept your fly. However, the way you approach a school of breaking fish can determine how long the fish will stay up and how many you can catch.

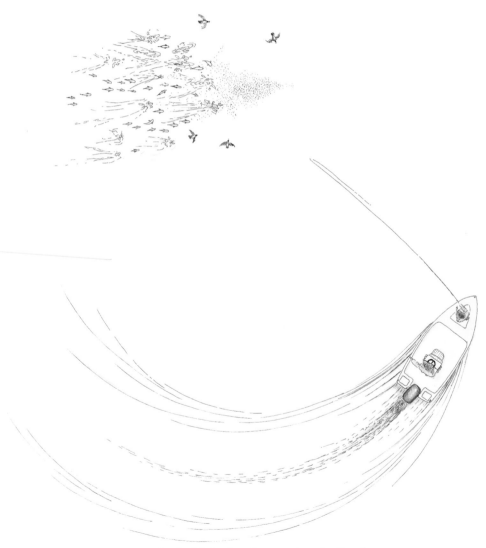

Don't run your boat over a school of fish when they are in a feeding frenzy.

The worst approach is to roar in and stop the boat in the middle of the school. It's like leaping into a flock of quail on the ground—they scatter in all directions. The best approach is to observe which way the school is moving from a distance and stop well ahead of that direction. Shut off the motor and wait for them to come to you. If that isn't possible, or many other boats are also working the fish, then motor ahead and to one side of the fish, then cast to them. If one person mans the boat and tries to stay within casting distance, but not so close as to alarm the school, you can get some great action.

Another factor is fly selection. Anglers often think because the fish are in a feeding frenzy, they will hit anything. Not true. Many times they are very selective. If you are not getting the strikes you think you should, try to match the size of the baitfish. Usually, a smaller fly will be more effective than a larger one.

Detecting Deep-Water Strikes

You need to learn how to detect strikes when fishing in deep water, because you can't see fish that may be taking your fly. Deep-water fishing would include fishing in channels where depths exceed 10 feet. It would also include the areas around wrecks, along the coral reefs, and around bridge pilings that are well below the surface. Chumming, where the fish may lie deep in the chum line and not near the surface, is another deep-water situation. Deep-water fishing requires more concentration than working the flats or shallows with a fly rod because you're fishing blind and relying on the sense of touch more than anything else.

Obviously, if a fish grabs the fly and takes off, much like a king mackerel or tuna would do, there is no doubt that you have a fish on. But when you are fishing in water more than 10 feet deep, and a soft take occurs, how do you know? Fortunately, there are some tips that will help you.

First, you must select the proper fly line. For many years, weight-forward sinking fly lines were constructed much like floating weight-forward fly lines. There was a short level section (usually a foot in length) at the front end, called the tip. Then the line gradually increased in diameter for 6 to 10 feet (called the front taper). This was followed by the heavy belly section. The line then began reducing in diameter over 7 to 10 feet (called the back taper), and then came the running line, which was a long level line that aided in shooting the head farther.

The problem was that the heaviest portion sank faster than the rest of the line, so the tip and front taper were sinking at a slower rate. The leader and fly were higher in the water than the heavier belly section. The fly line, leader, and fly during the retrieve resembled a shallow U, with the belly well below the fly. When a fish took the fly, the angler wasn't aware of the take until the sag was pulled from the U shape in the line. Fortunately, weight-forward sinking lines now have a belly and tip that sink at the same rate because the line is the same diameter all the way to the tip.

The obvious advantage to this type of line is that all of the line is fairly taut, and when a fish takes the fly, the angler immediately feels a strike.

Leaders must be considered also, because they don't sink as fast as the line, so you often get a lofting of the fly. This can delay the message to the angler that the fish has taken the fly. Most fish are not as leader shy when they are deep under water, and you don't have to worry about line impact on the surface.

Leaders for sinking lines should be fairly short so that when the fish strikes, it is immediately evident.

One trick that aids in detecting underwater strikes, even when fishing a floating line in 4 or more feet of water, is to place the rod tip underwater during the retrieve. Leave the rod tip under the water as you retrieve until you feel a wet line passing over your stripping finger. I can't explain why, but the wet line gives you a more sensitive contact with the fly.

Another tip that I often use when fishing flies deep is to run a small amount of silicone paste, such as line dressing, in the groove of my finger where the line is being stripped across. This permits me to feel the line much better and I can detect soft strikes much more easily.

Teasing Fish to Your Fly

There are times when fish are simply reluctant to strike our flies, but you can "excite" some fish into striking without using a chum line.

Use a Chugger

Whenever possible, you should include a spinning rod in your fishing arsenal to excite and stimulate the fish with a chugger. A chugger is simply a surface lure with a cupped face and no hooks. It should be about 3 inches in length and ¾ to 1 inch in diameter. Chuggers are widely available, but you can also make your own. Get a wooden dowel about ¾ to 1 inch in diameter and about 2½ to 3 inches in length. Use a grinding tool to make a depressed cup in the face of the lure. About ¾ inch behind the cup, taper the lure so that the back end is a bit smaller than the front. Add a stout screw eye to the center of the cupped area and another screw eye at the rear. Attach a ⅛- to ¼-ounce sinker on the rear screw eye. The sinker will cause the rear of the chugger to dip downward when the lure is at rest. It will also make more noise and make the chugger easier to cast.

Many fish won't respond to a streamer that swims silently through the water. Others will look at a streamer, but won't attack it, because they aren't excited. The chugger can often provoke the fish into hitting your offering.

To use the chugger, you need a companion who will cast the chugger with the spinning rod into an area where fish are likely to be holding. You should be ready to

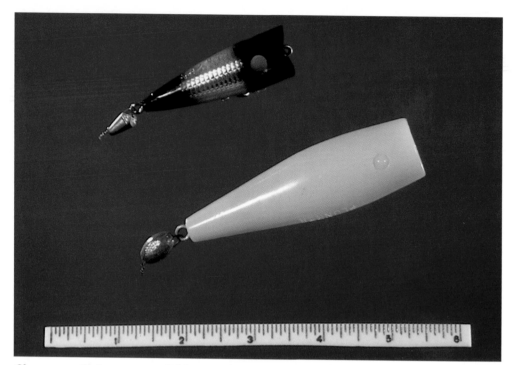

Chuggers will draw a gamefish's attention, convince it that there is feeding activity, and drive it to aggressive action.

cast with your fly rod when the opportunity occurs. When your partner flips the rod tip quickly, the chugger makes a loud "blooping" sound, dances on the surface, and creates a constant series of loud splashes. This surface activity causes fish to attack the hookless lure. Frequently, a fish will grab the lure several times because it is so excited. It ignores the fact that the lure is not naturally soft or yielding. When the fish is within casting range, the fisherman presents his fly as close to the chugger as possible. The chugger is then stopped dead in the water, and the fish will usually attack the fly when it swims by. If it doesn't strike, cast the fly again and repeat the procedure.

Small chuggers particularly excite ladyfish, which inhabit many tropical waters. A big ladyfish is perhaps 2 or 3 pounds, so a smaller chugger and a streamer of about 2 inches usually works well. Chuggers will also work on striped bass, jack crevalle, and bluefish. Large cobia will frequently ignore a streamer because their prey are usually larger baitfish. But when you toss a chugger to a cobia, it can provoke the fish to the point that it will take a streamer that it would usually ignore. Another occasion where the chugger is helpful is when there is a slack tide around a channel marker or buoy. Cobia, snook, triple tail, jewfish, and other species lie deep beneath the marker or buoy, and a chugger will often pull the fish to the surface, where you can get a shot at them.

Chuggers can be also used to lure fish *away* from markers and buoys. Because markers are encrusted in barnacles, chains, and other line-cutting hazards, it is best to lure the fish away before making the cast.

Several guides I know won't go out without a chugger outfit in the boat, and they claim that it has often saved the day for them. In short, chuggers can be used in many situations to cause a reluctant fish to readily strike your offering.

Use a Popping Bug/Streamer Combination

Another method to tease and excite fish is to use a Popping Bug in combination with a fly. The bug should be small enough so that it is easy to cast. Because a fly is

A Popping Bug and underwater fly combination.

Del Brown trails his line as Steve Huff poles. If a fish presents itself, Del won't need to backcast.

Flats Boats

Although you can certainly fish the flats without a boat, you must cover a lot of water to locate quarry. That calls for the use of a boat. There are all sorts of tricks to fishing from boats, ranging from how much fly line you drop on the deck to never casting directly ahead if you want to stay friendly with the fellow at the stern.

You'll have more fun and catch more fish on a flats boat if you and your companion work as a team. While one stands on the platform, ready to throw to the next fish, the other should be just as busy, maybe more so.

A major problem for the person casting on the bow is that they must keep the line free of tangles and obstructions. Because the fly fisherman concentrates on seeing fish and making good presentations, he is often unaware of the disasters that lurk nearby. The wind will blow the line around, it can slide underfoot, or it can catch on a rod holder or a piece of gear in the boat and spoil a cast. The companion can observe what is happening to the line and make sure that it stays tangle free.

If the angler breaks off his fish during a fight, or if a pattern isn't drawing strikes and a change in flies is needed, the companion can have additional flies and leader material ready. It is much quicker for the companion to replace the leader than the caster standing on the bow. It's also a good practice to check the hook point

When fishing on a flats boat, the companion will often stand on a platform in order to see fish and pole more effectively.

Keep your partner's line tangle free before he or she loses a fish.

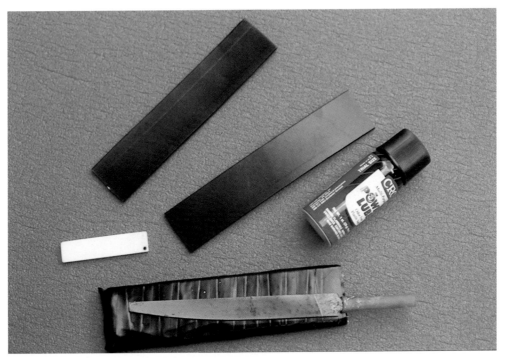

Keep a file handy to sharpen your partner's hook.

for sharpness after you miss more than two strikes. If the person sitting behind the caster has a file ready, the hook can be checked and honed in seconds.

If a fish is hooked and a knot develops in the line, the companion often has time to get the knot out before the fish pulls the line to the guides and snaps the fly off. There have been several times when either my friend or I saved a fish by such quick action. If a fish is hooked in rough water, the friend can often step to the platform and help stabilize the fisherman as he fights his quarry.

Many fish are difficult to see on a flat. A snook hiding among mangrove roots can be nearly impossible to spot. Despite its size, a permit can often be difficult to see—even for a guide on a poling platform. There are many indicators that help locate a fish on the flats. The guide and the angler look for all of these indicators, but so can the companion. The person who is not fishing is often the first to locate a fish.

The guide usually stands on the poling platform, which is elevated above the deck. When the angler hooks a fish and brings it to the boat, the guide must stow the pole and climb off the platform to land the fish. All of this takes time, during which the boat is not under control. Instead, the guide can maintain the boat if the companion will land the fish for his friend.

Once the fish has been landed, the angler often wants a photograph. Many guides, especially outside the United States, know little or nothing about photography. This is where a friend can really help out.

The fly cemetery.

Several years ago I began to carry a fly swatter on flats boats. The biting flies in Florida and the tropics really hurt. These stinging bloodsuckers have caused many fish to escape because anglers are distracted by their irritating bites as they try to present a fly or play a fish. Some of these flies are tough. I have knocked them unconscious with my hat, only to see them revive later, bite me, and then fly away. But your fishing partner can be ready with a fly swatter. Not long ago Mike O'Brien and I killed so many flies with my swatter that we actually wore it out. I piled a big number of their carcasses on the deck beside his feet, laid the ruined swatter beside it, and took a picture of what I called a "fly cemetery." There is also a certain satisfaction in killing them.

I have seen many pairs of fly fishermen in a flats boat. One stands on the platform, ready to fish. The other person simply sits back and relaxes. But the person who becomes a team player will get more fun out of the day, and both of them will probably catch more fish.

Flats and Backcountry Tips

There are also a number of dos and don'ts when fly fishing shallow saltwater flats and backcountry. The following tips can help you see fish better and quicker, cast to them more efficiently, and hook up more. Some of these tips also apply to freshwater fishing, but they are especially vital when seeking saltwater species in the shallows and the backcountry.

Use sharp hooks. Constantly check to make sure your hooks are sharp. It is much more important when fishing in salt water because so many saltwater species have really tough mouths.

Don't pull off too much line. Some anglers pull off 50 to 70 feet of line and drop it to the deck. Never pull off more line than you expect to cast. Surer than tomorrow, you'll be standing on it when you cast or when a fish begins its run. I like to put a long indicator mark with a waterproof pen on the line to show how much line I need to pull from the reel.

When fishing from the bow, always strip line off, make a cast, and retrieve the line. If you don't do this, the forward portion of your line will be on the bottom of the pile on the deck. When you cast, the line will feed from the bottom of the pile, which will result in tangles. Pull off the required amount of line and make a cast. When you strip in, the rear portion of the line will be on the bottom, where it belongs.

Be quiet when in a boat. The sounds that tackle boxes and feet make as they scrape along a deck will alarm fish. Try to be as quiet as possible when moving any items or yourself.

Don't speak loudly or yell when fishing in water less than a foot deep. Loud talking doesn't seem to affect fish when you are in deeper water. But my experience has been that yelling or talking loudly in very shallow water will alert fish to your presence.

Wear shoes with small strings or wear slip-ons. The worst offenders are moccasins that have those line-grabbing leather strings. There are a huge number of fish that never saw the fly because the angler tangled the fly line in his shoestrings when he attempted to cast. Florida Keys guides now charge about $400 or more a day. Some days you may only get shots at four tarpon. If your line tangles in your shoestrings on three of your four casts, you need to address the problem. The best solution is to use elastic to replace shoestrings.

Use short leaders on windy days and long leaders on calm days. It is nearly impossible to properly present a fly to a fish when the wind is blowing hard and you use a long leader. A short leader will spook fish on calm days.

Take your time to cast only as far as you comfortably can. Regardless of how frantic your guide or companion becomes, never cast farther than you can with confidence, and never rush your cast. This always results in a poor presentation. You may be surprised how much difference there is between a rushed cast and one when you take your time to do it well.

Wait until you see the fish before you cast. Casting to fish that you can't see almost always results in spooked fish, a spoiled presentation, or another cast. You should see the fish clearly before you throw the fly. The best way to quickly locate a fish that your guide is trying to show you is to learn the clock method and then move the rod to whatever time he says. For example, if he yells, "Bonefish at 10 o'clock," move your rod to what is 10 o'clock for you. If you can't see the fish, ask the guide to tell you whether you should point the rod left or right. This is the fastest way for you to locate a fish that someone else is trying to show you.

Don't cast your fly into the middle of a school of fish. Instead, throw your fly to the front of the school. That way, if the first target refuses your offering, another behind it may take the fly.

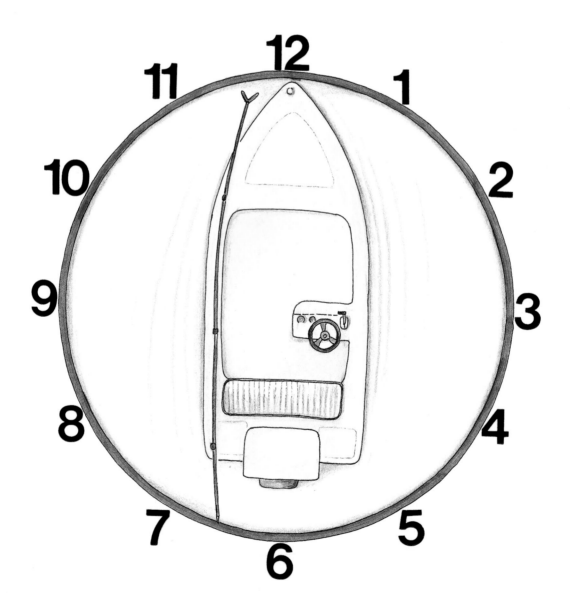

This angler is using the fly rod to determine where her guide has seen a fish.

Don't cast well above the water when throwing into the wind. This will cause the leader to fall back on the line at the end of the cast. When casting into the wind, aim toward the surface so that the moment the leader has unrolled, the fly will contact the water and won't be blown backward.

Cast above the surface when the wind and water are calm. Any disturbance on calm water will alert fish. A major mistake that many fresh- and saltwater fly fishermen make is to aim their casts at the water. Driving the fly at the surface can often mean a heavy splashdown. Instead, imagine that the water is at eye level. This will cause the fly to unroll above the target and the line and the fly will fall softly to the surface.

Don't let the fly contact the surface while false casting. This is especially important on the forward cast. I've watched many fish spook, especially bonefish, because the fly struck the surface between the angler and the boat. It is one of the most common reasons that novice anglers fail to catch bonefish.

Keep control of the line as you shoot it to the target. Bonefish and many other species are difficult to see. If you release the line as you cast when you finally locate the fish, you may have to take your eyes from the fish to find the line before retrieving. That shift of focus when you look away often makes it so that you can't relocate the fish, and disaster follows.

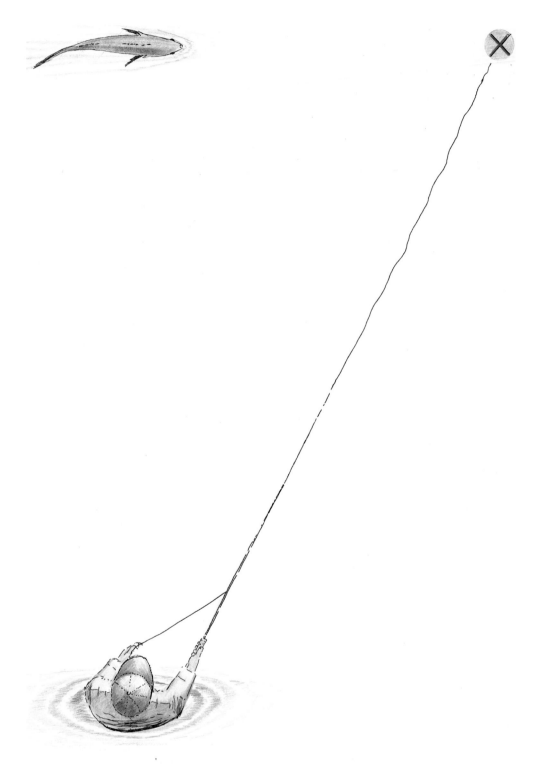

Be sure to cast well ahead of a cruising fish. This will allow the fly to sink to the appropriate level before the retrieve, and ensure that the fly will be placed where the fish can see it.

Don't present the fly close to gamefish that are especially wary. The best method to catch a spooky cruising fish is to select a place well in front of it and toss your fly there. Try to throw the fly to an easily identifiable object on the bottom. It could be a sea cucumber, a piece of coral, or a small patch of grass. Watch the fish as it approaches the predetermined spot where the fly is located and begin very short retrieves. If subtle movements don't work, give one or two quick strips, then switch back to slow strips. This will usually entice the fish into striking.

Master a number of different retrieves. Many anglers use a special retrieve for each fish species. Also, if your fly imitates a certain creature, you should mimic that creature's natural swimming motion; a mullet doesn't swim like a shrimp or a squid. This is particularly true when seeking bonefish. Perhaps 80 percent of the time, the fly should be presented as close as possible without alerting a fish—about 6 to 10 feet in front of the fish. If you're fishing for bonefish and you think that the fish detected the fly as it entered the water, make one or two long, quick strips, then let the fly drop toward the bottom. As the fish moves in, make a series of short strips, and let the fly rest momentarily on the bottom. If it is a redfish, permit, bonefish, or other bottom feeder, most of the time the fly is best worked on or near the sea floor. There are a very few occasions when it is a good idea to simply throw the fly in front of the bonefish and allow it to sink to the bottom before making a retrieve. Try one method, and then another, until you find what works in the area where you are fishing.

Vary your retrieve if the fish just follows the fly. There are almost no hard and fast rules about retrieving any underwater fly, but one rule that I live by is that if the fish closely follows any fly for more than 6 feet and it hasn't struck, I change the retrieve.

If the fish has moved away or it obviously hasn't seen the fly, pick up and make another quick cast. Freshwater fly fishermen new to salt water often believe that once a retrieve is started, it should be completed before you recast. The window of opportunity in saltwater fishing is brief, and you must use every opportunity as quickly as you can. The instant you realize that the fish is leaving the fly or hasn't seen it, pick the fly up and make another quick presentation.

Almost never work the fly with the rod tip. There are rare cases when jack crevalle, Spanish mackerel, king mackerel, wahoo, or barracuda will hit a fly if the rod is swept backward, which pulls the fly at great speed away from the fish. But these instances are rare, and you should almost never use the rod to manipulate the fly. Instead, point the rod low and toward the fish as you begin your retrieve, and use short, long, slow, and fast strips with your line hand to move your fly. This keeps the line taut, and if a fish strikes, you enhance your chances for a hookup.

Hold your rod low to the water while retrieving the fly. There are several reasons for doing this. If the tip is held well above surface, there will be a lot of sag in the line, which makes it more difficult for the angler to know when the fish has taken the fly. Another reason is that if the line is sagging, you must remove the slack before

Hold the rod tip close to the water on the retrieve.

the hook can be set. A third reason is that if wind is blowing from the side and against the line, the fly will be dragged along the bottom, which will spoil the retrieve.

Always lift the line quietly from the water. If I were to name one of the most common mistakes that even good fly fishermen make when fishing for shallow-water species, it's that they'll make a backcast before all the fly line is lifted from the water. Any line that remains on water is held there by surface tension, which requires effort to release it, and this steals energy from the cast. Worse, to a nearby fish, ripping the line from the surface is similar to someone standing on a corrugated roof and dragging a nail across the corrugations.

Wade slowly. Anglers tend to rush forward into a huge flat. But fast wading produces shock waves that are easily detected by wily fish. Remember, water transmits sound about 4½ times as fast as does air. If you see ripples moving more than a foot away from your legs when wading in knee-deep water, you are probably wading too fast.

Don't lift your feet when wading in tropical flats. Stingrays move onto a flat and pound their wings on the bottom to produce a cloud of silt and dirt. When they drop to the bottom, they allow the cloud of silt to fall over them. This camouflages them so well that they are nearly impossible to see. If you step on a hidden ray, it will try to drive its stinger tail into your leg. This is an extremely painful wound that

Lifting the line abruptly will cause a disturbance in the water.

Lift the line slowly on the back cast until the water tension releases it.

Slide your feet along the bottom when wading to avoid stingrays.

often requires hospital treatment. But there is no danger if you follow a simple rule. Never lift your feet from the bottom to walk in a normal manner when wading a tropical flat. Instead, slide your foot along the bottom. Rays are not aggressive, and if your foot touches the ray as you shuffle along, it will flee. But if you step on a ray, it will strike back.

Wade with the sunlight at your back if possible. Glare produced by the sun makes it extremely difficult to see fish. Try to select a portion of the flat that allows you to wade with the sun at your back or to the rear and one side.

When possible, wade with the wind. Wading with the wind blowing toward you means you'll have to direct your cast into the breeze, which is always difficult.

Don't wade or pole toward a white cloud. The reflection of the cloud will turn the surface pure white, which makes it impossible to see any fish below. Instead, wade or pole toward where there is a dark shoreline or a dark storm in the background. The background will reduce glare and you will be able to see the bottom and any fish moving on it.

Don't strike upward in shallow water. If you see a fish attack your fly, and you think that you have a fish on, never sweep the rod upward. If the fish missed the fly, an upward sweep of the rod will remove the fly from the water. If the fish is close, another cast may mean a spooked fish. Instead, set the hook by moving the rod side-

A dark storm in the background will allow you to see fish more effectively.

ways, or grip the line firmly and make a drawing motion away from the fish. If you miss a fish with either a slight side rod movement or strip strike, the fly will remain on the bottom and close to the fish.

Strike gently when setting the hook on bonefish or permit. All you need do is grip the fly line and gently move the rod tip to the side, or grip the line and slowly pull back gently to set the hook. Bonefish and permit are especially nervous, and the moment the steel is driven home, they go crazy. If you make a hard strike away from the fish, and the fish bolts in the opposite direction, the chances for breaking the tippet are magnified.

Straighten the fly line before you begin fishing. Many of the fly lines today will lie on the deck in tight coils when you pull them from the reel. You must remove the coils or you will almost certainly have a cast that ends in disaster. When you are in a boat, one of the quickest and easiest ways to do this is to simply pull off 8 or 10 feet of line and place the foot inside the loop and pull firmly on both ends. This way you can stretch the coils from a line in a hurry.

Don't use the same type of fly line for all your inshore fishing. If you are sight fishing for bonefish or tarpon, you may want a fly line that has a short taper, which allows you to get into action fast. But if you are searching for many other species in the shallows, where a long retrieve is profitable, then a shooting taper is best. If the surf is rough, a sinking line or slow-sinking line is better than a floating line. A floating line will undulate with the waves and give your fly poor action and unwanted slack. A sinking line will penetrate the water and remain relatively unaffected by the waves. On windy days, a slow- or fast-sinking line will let you throw a thinner diameter line. This will cast much better than a floating line. On very calm days, many anglers do better on spooky fish by using a lighter rod and line to reduce line impact on the water. In short, tailor your line to the existing conditions, and don't be afraid to change quickly.

III. FISH

CHAPTER 11

Striped Bass

Because of changes in conservation and fisheries management, striped bass have staged and incredible comeback in the eastern United States and have become the number-one target for many fly fishermen from Maine to South Carolina. There is also good striper fishing in the Delta area of San Francisco. Some of us have fished for stripers for years, but there are a host of newcomers who want to know more about pursuing this grand fish. In fact, the number of anglers fly fishing for stripers is growing faster than for any other saltwater species.

The following are some guidelines you can use to successfully catch striped bass anywhere they are found. All rules have exceptions, but the following tips will prove to be true most of the time.

Beaches

One of the advantages of fishing a beach is that you only need a minimal amount of specialized equipment. Unless the ocean is very warm, you should have a good pair of chest-high waders and a rain suit with a hood. Dropping your line in the surf can become a constant problem when casting, so some type of stripping basket is necessary. Floating lines are most popular for fishing the beaches, but many anglers are beginning to favor intermediate- or slow-sinking lines. Striped bass will

Chest waders, a rain suit with a hood, and a stripping basket can eliminate frustration and discomfort.

often hold at varying depths, especially in the summer, when the fish generally tend to be much deeper. To reach these fish, you will need to carry floating and fast-sinking lines. Some beaches have deeper water close to shore, and when there is a good bit of surf, it is often best to switch from a floating line to a faster-sinking type, such as a Teeny 300- to 450-grain line. The sinking lines offer a distinct advantage in rough surf. A floating line rides on top of the waves and can spoil your retrieve. A sinking line dives below the surface and allows a straight-line retrieve.

Structure

Beaches don't just taper up smoothly from the sea. The average beach has depressions in it, underwater sandbars, troughs, and other features. Depressions will trap baitfish as the waves move in and out, and that's where you'll find the most stripers. It pays to learn the topography of any beach you will fish. The very best time to do this is a spring low tide, during a new or full moon.

Underwater bars lying off the beaches are often superior places to fish when the tide flows across them. Many can be waded. The hot spot is on the downtide side because the bar forms a vertical eddy that traps crab, squid, and baitfish as water pours over it. I have had great success wading along a shallow bar and dropping a fly on the downtide side of the bar. These bars can be located if you prowl the beaches on extra-low spring tides. Often it's wise to photograph them when they protrude above the surface, so you know where to fish when you return.

Anywhere the current crashes against rocky structure is a potential hot spot for stripers. Bait is swept in with the crashing waves. But don't just cast to the walls. Study how they are formed. The structure of how the rocks are piled together is a tip-off. For example, when there are two huge rocks that form a wide, V-shaped opening at the top, but are joined at the base, you have a hot spot. The waves are thrown against the rocks. As the water rushes back, it flows down the V. Any bait carried with the water will be concentrated at the base of the V. Here's another example of evaluating where to cast to rocky structures: If a rock sits seaward of a rocky wall and water is trapped momentarily between the rock and the rocky shoreline as the water sweeps back to the sea, this spot will almost always hold bait, as well as a bass or two.

If a jetty juts out from the beach, you have a fishing spot with great potential. Jetties require special shoes that have rock-grabbing cleats. A wading staff is also helpful. Of all the places a shorebound fly fishermen can get into trouble, it's on a jetty. Be alert at all times for crashing waves, and above all, keep an eye on the rising tide. Many busy anglers have found that the path they came out on is now flooded, and they are stranded. Always fish a jetty with a companion, especially at night. Although rare, accidents can happen.

If a small bay or river connects to the sea through the beach, you have a great place to catch stripers. The very best time to fish such locations is when the tide is

A small V in the structure traps bait here as the tide rushes in and drains out.

outgoing. The bait that moved up the river or into the bay will be carried back to sea on the falling tide. By fishing throughout the falling tide, you have a great chance of scoring.

Water

Newcomers to fly fishing on the beaches often think that the tidal current sweeps in directly against the shoreline and then back again. On most shorelines, the tidal flow is *along* the beach, not in and out. Awareness of the direction of the tidal flow will tell you where the bait is being transported and how to fish your flies. Retrieving or dead drifting the fly with the current is advisable, because your fly goes in the same direction that baitfish would be carried along. A little chop or wave action is often better than a totally flat sea, because it gives the fly more action. It is also better to fish while the tide is flowing, because it concentrates baitfish and other morsels that stripers eat and carries them along. A slack tide will do the opposite. Stripers prefer the food to come to them.

The tide is also important when it creates eddies and tide rips (two forces of water smashing against each other) or when it comes into a narrows (such as water flowing out of the mouth of a bay). Fishing in any of these places at the right time

Two bodies of water at different speeds or temperatures have come together here to form a well-defined tide rip.

will increase your chances of catching fish. Stripers holding in a large eddy will often face different directions. The fish will face into the current, so plan your retrieve so that the fly comes to the fish as it would naturally.

Striped bass seem to be highly sensitive to bright sunlight, especially if the water is clear. Many people think stripers don't feed as well when there is a high-pressure system moving through. I believe it's not barometric pressure that affects them. I think they feed better during a low-pressure system or cold front because it brings rain, nasty weather, and reduced light.

A scientist once told me that a fish that descends 18 inches in the water has a barometric change on its body that would be about the same as going from a high-pressure system to a hurricane. This supports my belief that the intensity of the light has much greater influence on successful fishing than the barometric pressure. Foggy, rainy, and overcast days have almost always produced more fish for me.

Many anglers don't realize that striped bass will often move up on very shallow flats—less than 3 feet of water—during the daytime. They are wary and tough to stalk, but they can deliver some exciting fishing. (This is an excellent place to cast a crab pattern.)

Flies

Look for baitfish—it's one of your most important keys. If you see swirls or bait leaping from the water, move quickly to the area and cast. If you know stripers are feeding and they are not hitting your offering, try offering larger or smaller streamers. I believe striped bass are among the most particular species about fly size. If you are casting to fish and not getting hits, match your fly to the size of the baitfish in the area. Many times varying the fly length by a few inches can make a difference.

When a striped bass refuses a streamer, switch to a Popping Bug, which is one of the best flies to throw to striped bass. I think Popping Bugs tend to cause fish to believe that the offering is larger than it is because they produce a lot of noise and surface disturbance. But remember that a loud popper will frequently alarm fish on very calm days, so work it quietly or use a Slider.

Chartreuse is a color that stripers seem to be attracted to. Two flies I am never without are the Lefty's Deceiver and the Clouser Minnow, each with a liberal amount of chartreuse in them. Tie the flies in different lengths. You can fish the Clousers at various depths of the water if you use different size eyes.

Many fly fishermen tend to retrieve their flies too rapidly. There are times when a dead-drifted fly works much better. The Lefty's Deceiver is a good pattern to use. To prevent excessive drag, so the fly drifts naturally with the current, I often use a reach cast. You can find instructions for it in a number of fly-casting books.

One of the best fly patterns for striped bass is the crab pattern (I prefer Del Brown's Crab Fly). Live-bait fishermen know that a free-drifted crab on a hook is

A striper caught on a chartreuse fly.

something a striper can't resist. You should carry crab patterns that float, sink slowly, and sink quickly. It isn't necessary to have large flies; stripers eagerly take crab patterns as small as a 25-cent coin.

Boats

Fishing from a boat gives you the tremendous advantage of maneuverability. If you see birds circling and diving close to the water, a fast boat can be on the scene in no time. It pays not to run into the school of breaking fish, but try to estimate their direction and stop the boat in front and to one side of them. Running through the school often puts the fish down. And, it's always best for the operator to position the boat on the upwind side, giving the fly caster a better chance to throw the fly.

Hot Spots

Some of the very best places to fish for stripers are where waves crash against the shoreline (especially if they come out of deep water) or just off the beach where underwater troughs have trapped the bait and are too far out for shorebound casters

Boats allow you to cast to areas where shore fishermen can't reach.

to reach. A boat lets you roam, moving quickly from one site to another, seeking breaking fish, circling birds, or any evidence of stripers. Another tremendous advantage for anyone in a boat is the use of a depth finder. After 2 years of using a depth finder equipped with both vertical and side finder readings, I am convinced that this is the way to go. On a number of occasions, the horizontal side transducer has shown fish we would never have known about with only a vertical finder.

One of the best all-year fishing spots for stripers in some waters are power plants. A huge amount of bait is sucked into power plants, chewed up, and spewed out with warm water from the generators to form a gigantic chum line. Boats allow you to get to and fish effectively at power plants.

Chumming

Chumming is another deadly way to catch striped bass. Instead of chasing them, you lure them to boatside. Ground menhaden, clams, or other bait is fed overboard slowly, which attracts striped bass. If you are using ground chum, a fly I developed some years ago is deadly effective. I call it Chum Fly Bloody. It is often as effective as a hunk of chum meat impaled on a hook. Tie some dark brown marabou on the underside and then the top of a size 1, 1/0, or 2/0 hook. The marabou should

Here is a terrific example of what striped-bass fishing has to offer.

Bluefish are aggressive and voracious.

one place to the next, but if you chum, this will be less of a problem. The blues will try to stay in the area as long as there is a promise of food.

There are several ways to chum for bluefish, but the most successful along the mid-Atlantic and northeastern coast of the United States is with ground baitfish. Menhaden or bunker are baitfish whose bodies contain large quantities of oil. When they are ground and dribbled overboard, they create an oily slick that tantalizes blues. Nothing pulls bluefish into a chum line as quickly as fresh ground bunker. Another baitfish that is excellent for chum is the alewife, which is a favorite natural prey of bluefish. Although chumming is practiced effectively up and down the coast, the best operations are in the Chesapeake Bay off the coast of Delaware, in New Jersey, and along the shores of Long Island in New York.

Many people will gather scraps of fish or catch large numbers of baitfish in a net, grind them up, and freeze them in cardboard cartons for later use. Ground baitfish can be stored in a freezer for a long time and is often available from many tackle shops. When you want to use it, the chum is suspended overboard in a mesh sack. I advise using a soft cord or rope when you attach it and hang it overboard. I once had a net bag of chum suspended a few feet from the transom of a boat when a shark grabbed the bag. We had a few nervous moments until the shark worked the bag loose from the line. You can also suspend a frozen chum block with a downrigger ball. Again, use soft rope or cord instead of wire to attach the chum to the ball, or you may lose the ball. The downrigger ball is a good device when fish are running deep and you want to draw them closer to the surface, where fly fishermen can get to them. Start off by dropping the ball down deep, with the chum bag attached. Then bring the bag slowly toward the surface. If bluefish have located the chum bag and are feeding on the melting morsels, they can be drawn up through the water column, until the bag is suspended just below the surface.

If you are using a frozen chum block in a bag in choppy water, the rise and fall of the boat will work off pieces of ground chum as the block thaws. But if the water is calm, the angler will have to bounce the bag up and down regularly to flush freshly thawed chum from the bag.

The most effective bluefish chummers prefer freshly ground chum. This requires a little more effort, but anyone who has much experience at chumming blues will tell you that it is vastly superior. A sausage grinder is used to

grind whatever baitfish are being used into small bits. While a small household-type grinder will work, a commercial sausage grinder is best because it will chew up any kind of baitfish you put through it. The grinder is usually attached to a board, which is secured to the side of the boat. You can hand grind your chum, but this can be a lot of work. Most commercial sausage grinders permit you to hook a slow-speed motor to the unit. The motors range from small lawn mower engines to the best of them all, an electric motor used to pull a boat on a trailer. This motor is relatively inexpensive, is built to stand saltwater corrosion, and runs at slow rpms off the battery in the boat.

Almost all experienced chummers agree that the fresher the baitfish, the better it draws in fish. If you live in an area where you know commercial fishermen that net bunker, alewives, and similar species, you can arrange to come by early in the morning and pick up several bushels of chum. On a day of 4 or 5 hours of chumming, you'll need 3 to 4 bushels of ground chum. The baitfish are put through the grinder and deposited in a pile on the board. Then start ladling out large soupspoonfuls.

Perhaps the most important aspect of chumming is that once you start chumming, don't stop. Don't overchum and waste meat, but if you chum too sparsely after

Albacore are fast and catching them can be exhilirating.

works best. Flies with synthetic wing materials seem to do better than more opaque materials, like bucktail, because they have excellent eyesight and roam clear waters.

You need a boat to locate and catch these fish. Once you have found them, you then race in front of the school and hope they will pass close by. Because they are usually pushing the bait to the surface, you don't have to fish deep. Just get the fly in front of them and retrieve quickly. Bob Popovics and Lance Erwin developed a deadly technique for large numbers of albacore. Use a small Popping Bug with a Surf Candy or Clouser Minnow as a dropper below the bug. Race ahead of the fish, stop the boat, and cast the popper with the fly suspended about 18 inches below. If there is a chop, you don't need to retrieve. Just hold the rod still and the waves will cause the popper and Clouser to bob up and down. If the surface is calm, just manipulate the popper gently. This technique will often outfish frequent casts and retrieves.

When the bonito or albacore aren't breaking the surface very often, or when there are only scattered schools around your boat, you can resort to a trick to keep them around you. Keep an ample supply of small frozen baitfish 2 to 3 inches in size. When albies or bonito are surfacing, immediately throw a few handfuls of the bait out on the water. If you keep a constant but not overly heavy flow of chum in the water, the fish will usually remain, and you'll increase your chances.

The best albacore fishing occurs during the last part of October and most of November at Cape Lookout, North Carolina. Tom Earnhardt took me there about 8

rigger ball is a good device when fish are running deep and you want to draw them closer to the surface, where fly fishermen can get to them. Start off by dropping the ball down deep, with the chum bag attached. Then bring the bag slowly toward the surface. If bluefish have located the chum bag and are feeding on the melting morsels, they can be drawn up through the water column, until the bag is suspended just below the surface.

If you are using a frozen chum block in a bag in choppy water, the rise and fall of the boat will work off pieces of ground chum as the block thaws. But if the water is calm, the angler will have to bounce the bag up and down regularly to flush freshly thawed chum from the bag.

The most effective bluefish chummers prefer freshly ground chum. This requires a little more effort, but anyone who has much experience at chumming blues will tell you that it is vastly superior. A sausage grinder is used to

grind whatever baitfish are being used into small bits. While a small household-type grinder will work, a commercial sausage grinder is best because it will chew up any kind of baitfish you put through it. The grinder is usually attached to a board, which is secured to the side of the boat. You can hand grind your chum, but this can be a lot of work. Most commercial sausage grinders permit you to hook a slow-speed motor to the unit. The motors range from small lawn mower engines to the best of them all, an electric motor used to pull a boat on a trailer. This motor is relatively inexpensive, is built to stand saltwater corrosion, and runs at slow rpms off the battery in the boat.

Almost all experienced chummers agree that the fresher the baitfish, the better it draws in fish. If you live in an area where you know commercial fishermen that net bunker, alewives, and similar species, you can arrange to come by early in the morning and pick up several bushels of chum. On a day of 4 or 5 hours of chumming, you'll need 3 to 4 bushels of ground chum. The baitfish are put through the grinder and deposited in a pile on the board. Then start ladling out large soupspoonfuls.

Perhaps the most important aspect of chumming is that once you start chumming, don't stop. Don't overchum and waste meat, but if you chum too sparsely after

Chumming in the Chesapeake Bay.

luring fish into your chum line or forget to continue chumming after you start catching fish, the fish will leave and you'll have to locate them again. There's no hard-and-fast rule about how fast or how much to chum. But within a minute after I see the chum sweep beyond the boat in the current, I like to throw another spoonful of chum overboard.

Floating lines do poorly in almost all chumming situations. What you really need is a sinking-tip line. A fast-sinking line is a good backup. Most of the time you can do well with just the sinking tip, but there are times when a fast-sinking line will be better.

Bluefish can range in size from 2 to 18 pounds. A 7- or 8-weight is the ideal rod size, but I have fought blues with a 5- or 6-weight rod on many occasions just for the fun of it. Fortunately, you don't have to cast far. Indeed, you don't want to cast!

When fishing a chum line for blues, or even tuna, barracudas, or sharks, *do not manipulate the fly.* What you want to do is imitate the drifting food particles that are

being used to lure the fish. The fly should match the color of the chum being fed to the fish, and it should travel at the same depth as the drifting chum. I like to use the Chum Fly Bloody mentioned in the previous chapter. Floating lines tend to carry your fly too high in the water, but if you use a sinking-tip line or a fast-sinking line (I like to carry two rods already rigged), you can keep the fly drifting at the correct depth as the chum rides high or low.

I can't stress how important it is not to manipulate the fly. Chum line fly fishing is much like fishing with nymphs for trout. You drop the fly at the point where the spoonfuls of chum are being thrown on the water and watch the line as it drifts. If the line stops, or moves in any manner except the natural drift, strike! Because the fly is drifting freely on a loose line, it's especially important to keep your hooks very sharp.

Use a short line—rarely more than 15 feet—and a leader from 1 to 2 feet in length. Because bluefish have very sharp teeth, you'll need to use wire. Some anglers maintain that heavy monofilament makes a good shock leader, and they often suggest 60-pound mono. I have lost almost every bluefish that exceeded 12 pounds that I hooked on monofilament, and I have used mono to 125-pound test. I use number 3 or 4 solid trolling wire no longer than the width of my hand as the shock leader. If the water is fairly clear, a wire leader more than 6 inches long will often discourage strikes.

One of the nice things about chumming for bluefish is that if you have no boat, or want to enjoy it with several friends, there are many places to charter boats from North Carolina and Virginia all the way to New England. Three or four people can easily fish the chum line at the same time, and you can split a charter with your friends. The skipper knows where the blues are, furnishes the bait, and does all the work, while you have all the fun.

CHAPTER 13

A Mixed Bag

There are several inshore species that are not as hard sought as stripers and bluefish, but still offer excellent fly-rod targets.

Seatrout

There are two common species of what are called saltwater trout. Spotted seatrout are found in the East from the Gulf Coast to Virginia. Gray trout, or weakfish, range from South Carolina to New England. These species are not actually trout, but are related to drum, and were in decline for many years. Both have bounced back. The spotted sea trout doesn't get as large as the weakfish. A trophy would weigh more than 6 pounds. I have caught weakfish to 9 pounds, though most will average 1 to 2 pounds.

The spotted seatrout usually inhabits saltwater basins that are 3 to 10 feet deep with a bottom containing a lot of grass. The grass will float on the surface because storms and the tide frequently tear it loose. This can interfere with your retrieve, so I recommend a weedless fly. Neither species is a strong swimmer, so they prefer to hold where food can be swept to them. Two surefire locations are where a slough drains water from a bay or where a river enters a larger bay on the falling tide.

The seatrout, or weakfish.

Larger weakfish tend to be nocturnal feeders, but spotted seatrout usually do not. They will feed at night near lighted boat docks and bridges if there is a good flow of tide, or wherever tidal currents will funnel baitfish to them.

The same flies work well for both species. They are easily attracted to a noisy Popping Bug, and the combination of the popper with a Clouser Minnow is deadly. Good baitfish imitations—such as Lefty's Deceiver and Surf Candy—work well and I know of no other saltwater fish that responds as well to fluorescent-colored flies, especially chartreuse, orange, and yellow, or a combination of two of these colors. Seatrout also like a lot of flash in the flies. A sinking line is advised for most fishing, unless the trout are in water less than 4 feet deep.

Bonito and Albacore

Bonito and albacore are two of the most exciting fish you can tangle with. They are speedy and can rip line from your reel in a hurry. You'll be able to see and identify them from their quick leaps as they catapult into the air to chase baitfish. You should use small and sleek flies for both of these species. Occasionally, large albacore will take flies like a Half & Half, but most of the time, a fly from 2½ to 4 inches in length

Albacore are fast and catching them can be exhilirating.

works best. Flies with synthetic wing materials seem to do better than more opaque materials, like bucktail, because they have excellent eyesight and roam clear waters.

You need a boat to locate and catch these fish. Once you have found them, you then race in front of the school and hope they will pass close by. Because they are usually pushing the bait to the surface, you don't have to fish deep. Just get the fly in front of them and retrieve quickly. Bob Popovics and Lance Erwin developed a deadly technique for large numbers of albacore. Use a small Popping Bug with a Surf Candy or Clouser Minnow as a dropper below the bug. Race ahead of the fish, stop the boat, and cast the popper with the fly suspended about 18 inches below. If there is a chop, you don't need to retrieve. Just hold the rod still and the waves will cause the popper and Clouser to bob up and down. If the surface is calm, just manipulate the popper gently. This technique will often outfish frequent casts and retrieves.

When the bonito or albacore aren't breaking the surface very often, or when there are only scattered schools around your boat, you can resort to a trick to keep them around you. Keep an ample supply of small frozen baitfish 2 to 3 inches in size. When albies or bonito are surfacing, immediately throw a few handfuls of the bait out on the water. If you keep a constant but not overly heavy flow of chum in the water, the fish will usually remain, and you'll increase your chances.

The best albacore fishing occurs during the last part of October and most of November at Cape Lookout, North Carolina. Tom Earnhardt took me there about 8

Bonito are often close to shore.

years before this writing. There were thousands of albacore (locally called albies, or Fat Alberts) roaming inside the bight and just outside. Scores of bottom fishermen were anchored everywhere, fishing for seatrout and croakers. Tom and I caught big albies until we simply gave up. As we fought and released the albacore, we could hear the locals commenting about how crazy we were to catch fish you couldn't eat, and then throw them back. That first year Tom and I were the only fly fishermen there. The next year we saw two other boats with fly fishermen. Then the word got out. Now Earnhardt and Donnie Jones have organized a gala albacore event in the first week of November, when several hundred fly fishermen descend on Harker's Island. Two years ago I counted 126 boats around the bight. There we so many albacore that almost every boat had at least one person fighting fish at any time. Not only are the albacore plentiful there at that time of year, but the average size is larger than elsewhere along the East Coast. It isn't unusual to catch albies of 16 or 17 pounds, and the largest I've seen taken on a fly weighed 21 pounds.

On rare occasions, when there aren't many albies thrashing the water at Cape Lookout, you can catch fish by following trawlers. The trawlers drag nets on the sea floor just outside the bight. Fly fishermen have found that by using fast-sinking lines and fishing deep behind the boat, they can often hook many albies. The nets must stir up considerable food. This is one place where a true trophy albie may

Albacore often congregate behind a trawler that is kicking up shrimp from the bottom.

Fishing behind these traulers can be extremely productive.

be caught, and it is a good idea to use slightly larger flies in this situation. I recommend the Half & Half.

Redfish and Bonefish

Of all species you can catch on a fly in fresh or salt water, the bonefish is my personal favorite. The techniques for redfish are essentially the same as for bonefish. Bones are usually found in clear water on flats that are firm and have no grass. Redfish will live on bonefish-type flats but are more frequently found where the bottom is softer and covered with grass and where the water is a little less clear. Both fish have small mouths located on the bottoms of their heads so that they can feed on the bottom. Flies that are longer than 3 inches are usually not as effective. Although redfish will try to take a surface fly such as a Dahlberg Diver or Popping Bug, underwater flies fished close to or on the bottom offer a better chance for a hookup.

If you are new to redfish or bonefish, 1 or 2 days with a competent guide are more than worth the money. Bonefish are as spooky as a cat in a dog pound. Redfish used to be less wary, but fishing pressure all along the coasts of Florida and the Gulf have made them as shy as bonefish. You need to make a quiet approach. I cast the fly at least 6 to 10 feet in front of a cruising bonefish and allow the fly to drop to the bot-

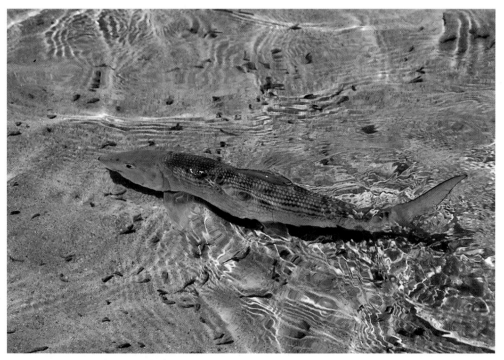

Bonefish are spooky and well-camouflaged.

Finning bonefish.

tom. I usually make two long strips with the fly to give the bonefish the impression that prey has seen it, and it is trying to escape. If the fish acts as if it has spotted the fly, I then begin alternating in short strips. As mentioned in Chapter 8, if the bonefish tracks the fly closely but doesn't strike, do something different. Often two or three fast, long strips will trigger a strike. I use a slower retrieve for redfish but essentially the same technique. The flies you use for bonefish and redfish should match the color of the flat. If bones are found on light-colored marl flats, then a cream, light tan, or pink fly is a good choice to start with. Most redfish are found where there is an abundance of grass on the flats—usually olive or tan—so a fly matching this grass color is best to start with. The only exception to this is a pattern that contains chartreuse.

I prefer a 12-foot leader for most bonefish situations. I'll shorten it to 10 feet on windy days, but on very calm days, when bonefish are exceptionally wary, I'll use a 16-foot leader. A 10- to 12-foot leader will suffice for redfish. Consult Chapter 4 to see how to build or modify your leader.

Bonefish and redfish can be tricky. Here is a typical fly-fishing scenario: A wading angler sees a 24-inch redfish facing away from him. The angler has a 3-inch shrimp fly on his leader. He makes a careful and quiet cast, being sure not to drop the fly line on the fish. The fly settles to the water so gently that the redfish is not alarmed, and the angler begins the retrieve. The fly approaches from directly in front

Catching bonefish requires patience and technique.

of the redfish. It sees a 3-inch shrimp attacking it. Naturally, it flushes away from something so unnatural.

What should he do? Whenever presenting a fly to a fish, try to have the fly and the fish come together in a natural manner. Let me give an example of what I think is the best of all approaches. If you have ever fished a river or tidal current, you usually make a cast across and slightly downstream. A retrieve is begun. Most of your strikes will come at the end, when the fly swings in a curve just before the line straightens. Why is this?

As your fly drifts downstream, it makes that looping curve just in front of a predator fish holding in the current. I think this is natural to the fish. Any baitfish or food for the predator that is drifting in the current must look downstream from it. If it sees the predator, it will attempt to swim to the side and away from the predator. The looping curve of the final part of your retrieve imitates that action—and that is why the fish strikes.

Let's take the redfish example cited earlier. Don't throw the fly so that when it is retrieved it attacks the fish. Instead, if the fly is cast a little to the side and in front of the fish, then a good retrieve can be made. As the fly swims back toward the angler, it is off to the side as though it were trying to sneak past, and the redfish is tempted to strike.

Large bonefish such as this can be caught in mangroves as well as on the flats.

Use the comfort grip when releasing bonefish.

Redfish live in many of the same waters as bonefish.

Tuna

Chumming works exceptionally well for tuna. During the summer and fall, various species of tuna move to the inshore waters of New England and the mid-Atlantic states. To keep them near the boat, cut fairly large pieces of fish (bonito are great, because they hold a lot of blood) and throw them overboard steadily. The tuna see the hunks of fish sinking in the water column and hang around for more. This very effective technique is called *chunking,* and it is also used in the tropical waters of Florida and the Bahamas to hold many excited and hungry species of fish near the boat.

Snook

Snook are ambushers and can be compared in many ways with largemouth and smallmouth bass. They prefer the same retrieves, and they like to hide in cover and explode quickly on their prey. Snook often hide under logs or back in the roots of mangroves. They are also found around channel markers and drainage ditches where a falling tide will deliver prey to them. You can fish for them at night around lighted docks and piers, where they come to feed on shrimp, baitfish, crabs, and other prey

Large redfish are caught among weedy flats.

Snook inhabit areas that have a lot of structure and vegetation. Use a weedless fly to catch them.

attracted to the lights. In spring, they roam the beaches along the coast to look for mates.

Many of the places where you fish for snook contain debris or vegetation that can snag your fly, so I recommend some type of weedless fly. The Bendback is a first choice for throwing around mangrove roots, docks, and piers. A second choice is to use a weedguard of some sort. As indicated earlier, the 40-pound-test, plastic-coated braided wire holds up better under hard fishing.

Many fly patterns work on snook, especially if they imitate local baitfish. Size is often critical. If they are feeding on tiny 2-inch glass minnows, a much larger fly will often be refused. Patterns that have been very effective for snook include the Seaducer (when you fish shallow water and want a fly you can retrieve very slowly), the Bendback, the Glades Deceiver (this is a Lefty's Deceiver about 3 inches in length with a weedguard), and Popping Bugs.

Permit

Many fly rodders consider permit to be the flats gamefish of choice. For many years, we simply didn't know how to catch them. It was finally determined that fly

Permit

patterns that imitated a crab, which is one of their favorite foods, was the trick. Although there are rare situations in which an unweighted crab pattern will work best, most of the time you want a fly that will get to the bottom quickly. Most crab flies have lead eyes located at one end to cause the fly to drop down fast. Because they have deep bodies, it is best to fish for permit during the higher spring tides, because it gives them a better opportunity to get up on the flats. They also tend to prowl along the channel edges of flats, especially on falling tides. Here they have the safety of deep water, but they can grab any prey that happens to float off the flat with the falling tide.

The technique that most experienced permit fly rodders use is rather simple. Once the permit is located, throw a Crab Fly 1 foot ahead of it. The fish will flee immediately at least half of the time, but some fish will show an interest as the fly drops quickly to the bottom. If the permit has seen the fly and shows interest, don't move the fly! If the fish hasn't seen it, a gentle nudge to barely move the fly is all that is required. If the permit circles the fly, don't move it. No natural crab is going to dance around on the bottom to attract the permit's notice. If the permit seems to be leaving, twitch the fly. If the permit continues to swim away, repeat the entire procedure. On several occasions I have had a permit take after three presentations, so don't give up.

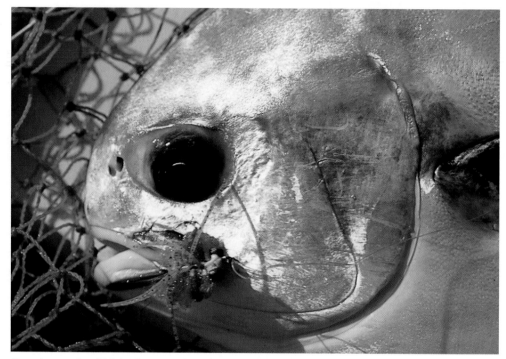

Permit are plentiful in the estuaries of the Yucatan Peninsula.

Tarpon

For many anglers, no fly rod target is as exciting as the tarpon—especially giant tarpon exceeding 160 pounds. Tackle for such giants is special. For many years a 12- or 13-weight rod and line were the most popular choices, but anglers found them difficult to cast. Because fly fishermen are now learning to fight big fish with the butt of the rod instead of the upper portion, many anglers now prefer either a 10- or 11-weight rod, which is more than strong enough to land a tarpon of less than 160 pounds.

Regardless of how you build your leader for giant tarpon, it should have a bite or shock leader of 80- to 110-pound monofilament at least 10 inches in length. The tarpon's mouth is very rough, and anything smaller will almost surely shear during the battle. For smaller tarpon to about 50 pounds, a 30- to 60-pound-test bite or shock leader is usually sufficient.

For many years, flies for tarpon were made in the Keys style. Four to six neck or saddle hackles were flared outward like a frog's legs beyond the bend of the hook, and some hackle was wound in front. The hook shank was left bare. Later, rabbit fur was substituted for the hackles in many patterns. But the giant tarpon in the Keys have grown wary of these flies. Today, the most effective patterns for large and small tarpon are more natural flies that imitate squid, baitfish, and crabs. Many years ago,

Tarpon are among the largest and most exciting saltwater prey.

Tarpon can make spectacular leaps and runs.

Landing a fish the size of a grown man can be quite an undertaking.

the hook size for giant tarpon was a 5/0, but the most popular size today is a 3/0. For smaller tarpon, hooks ranging from a size 2 to 2/0 are recommended. It's amazing how well small flies work on tarpon. A tarpon fly should rarely exceed 3 inches in length—even for a 150-pound fish.

The retrieve is a simple one. Like most predators, tarpon will rarely descend in the water to take a fly. Ideally, the cast should be directed to the front of the fish so that the fly is at the same depth as the fish at some time during the retrieve. Most of the time, medium-slow strips of a foot or more in length work well. If the tarpon tracks the fly but doesn't seem inclined to take, make a few long, fast strips and then go back to your normal retrieve. When a very large tarpon is hooked, it is better to set the hook several times, as long as the fish is not swimming away from you.

Barracuda

Many anglers thrill at the prospect of catching a barracuda because it has such a fierce reputation. This fish is so fast that once it attacks a prey, the baitfish rarely escapes. You can never retrieve a fly fast enough to deceive a 'cuda. So don't try.

I used the long, skinny patterns that resemble needlefish, a favorite food of 'cudas, for many years, but there are disadvantages to this fly. It frequently tangles dur-

Tarpon can often be seen rolling in the distance.

Barracuda are fast and ferocious predators.

ing a cast, which can ruin an opportunity. It also offers such a thin profile that sometimes I think 'cuda never see it. When fishing for 'cudas, you must accept two facts: that perhaps half of all your presentations will be ignored or cause them to flee, and that a 'cuda will almost never strike after it has been lured to a boat on a retrieve.

I favor a fly that is red over orange, or chartreuse over white, or a Popping Bug. The underwater flies work about half the time if you make a special retrieve. Once a 'cuda is located, approach close enough so that you make a forward cast with a weight-forward line, but pick up all the line you cast. Toss the fly about 6 to 10 feet in front of and just beyond the 'cuda. Lower the rod immediately, draw the fly through the water in front of the fish, and make a backcast. This will frighten at least half the 'cudas you throw to. But it seems to interest the rest, who apparently see something hit the water, streak past them, and

A barracuda is lurking in the foreground.

disappear. Repeat the same cast two more times. On the fourth cast, begin an erratic retrieve of the fly. It doesn't have to be moving fast, but it does have to be moving at all times! I have found this to be the most effective underwater retrieve for 'cudas. Many times a Popping Bug worked with a never-stopping retrieve is very effective. Because 'cudas have such good eyesight, I prefer using single-strand wire never more than 10 inches in length as a bite tippet.

Sharks

Sharks are one of the most difficult fish to catch on a fly rod. Very small bonnet and blacktop sharks will attack almost any fly as they cruise bonefish flats. But as sharks get bigger, they seem to get smarter—at least about taking flies. However, there is a surefire way to get a shark to hit your fly.

Barracudas respond to red over orange underwater flies.

Shark

Catch a small barracuda (the best fish to use as a decoy) or a catfish (which is very tough). But any small dead fish can be used. Attach the dead fish to a length of thin rope or line and let it drag behind the boat as you drift along in waters that sharks inhabit. The juices and scent from this fish are very apparent to any nearby shark, which will move in to grab your decoy. You must keep a careful watch on the fish or the shark may steal it.

When you see a shark near the decoy fish, get ready to cast. Orange/red or yellow/red flies appeal most to sharks, and they are easy to see. The decoy is removed immediately before the cast is made. It must be remembered that a shark's eyes are located well back on the head. If you cast directly in front of the shark, even if it sees the fly, the shark's nose may push it aside as it tries to grab your fly. You must cast the fly so that it lands and is retrieved near the eye of the shark. A shark strikes by sweeping its head to the side, so be ready for this. You'll need about 6 to 10 inches of wire connected to the fly or the shark's teeth will sever the leader. Don't use braided wire. Instead, use size 5 or 6 solid stainless steel trolling wire. Braided wire deteriorates during a battle as the shark goes through one strand and then another; finally, enough are severed so that the wire breaks.

Another method to draw sharks is to slowly pour concentrated fish oil and ground-up fish parts on the water. If there are any sharks in the area, they will usually show. This method works well in most cases, but not on a slack tide, because you need some current to broadcast the scent to the sharks.

Final Tips

Perhaps the most important difference between fishing in fresh water and fishing in salt water is that an angler working the salt has to be ready to function faster, more accurately, and more often. Readiness is the hallmark of an experienced saltwater fly fisherman, and it starts before you leave the house, motel, or camp.

Saltwater fly fishing demands sharper hooks. Freshwater fish have a relatively soft inner mouth, whereas many saltwater species have a mouth that seems tougher than a bank vault door. Instead of sharpening hooks just before you cast the fly, all hooks should be presharpened at home. Sometimes when a fish is hooked, the point is dulled or the fly is badly mangled during the fight. The fish is landed, but there are others nearby, hungry and eager to strike. This is no time to be sharpening hooks!

Spare leaders should be made beforehand and should be readily available in case the one on your line breaks. A heavy shock or bite leader attached in front of the fly must swim straight if the fly is to travel correctly on the retrieve. Most experienced tarpon fishermen know that getting the coils out of monofilament bite leaders with higher than 80-pound test is nearly impossible, so they prepare all their leaders ahead of time. The heavy monofilament is straightened, and the tippet and fly are attached. These completed and ready-to-use leaders and flies are stored in various types of containers so that the stiff monofilament remains straight. All you need do is lift one from its storage compartment and attach it to the butt section. For bluefish

Keep flies in waterproof, easy-to-see containers.

and barracuda, have a supply of flies with a short length of wire attached to each, ready to be tied to a leader.

Being ready means that when you arrive at a destination, your fishing tackle also gets there. Many experienced fly fishermen are now buying three- or four-piece rods that are carried inside protective tubes. The outside covering on the tubes often has a pouch where you can carry your reels, flies, leaders, and pliers. Because the carrying case is short, it can be taken on an airplane and stored overhead. When you walk off the plane, you know you have what you need to fish.

Pliers should always be on your hip, where they'll be instantly available if you should need them. They are indispensable for tightening knots, cutting wire or heavy monofilament, removing hooks from fish with razorlike teeth, and many other chores. If you have them stashed away, it may take too long to get them.

Rain can descend on you in a hurry when fishing in the salt, especially in the tropics. It always boggles my mind to see people go on any kind of saltwater fly-fishing trip and not carry rain gear. If there is one thing that every angler should have in addition to the tackle, it's good rain gear. I prefer separate jacket and pants. The jacket can be slipped on as a wind breaker, and the two-piece suit usually gives you more freedom of movement. Keep rain gear where you can grab it quickly. I've seen people keep rain gear in the bottom of their carrying bag, where it is difficult to get to.

Rod carrying cases keep your rods safe. Soft baggage pouches carry reels and other supplies and allow you to keep track of everything.

Nothing is more uncomfortable than hours of cold rain with no rain gear. Rain gear also acts as an effective windbreaker.

Wear a hat that clips to your shirt collar or has a stout chinstrap.

Every saltwater fisherman who has sped along in a boat has also had his cap fly off and into the water. You know it's going to happen, so be ready with a dry spare. Many people buy a hat that has a lanyard that clips from the hat to their shirt collar, or they will wear a hat with a chin strap. Never answer yes by nodding your head up and down while wearing a hat and cruising at high speed. I try to keep my head tilted forward so that the wind keeps the hat pushed tightly on my head.

Polarized glasses are an essential piece of your fishing tackle. If you have only one pair, especially on a distant trip, and you break or lose them, your fishing is going to be tougher. Carry a spare pair. If you wear prescription glasses and can't afford a second pair, at least carry a pair of clip-ons for your regular glasses. Clip-ons come in several tinted colors.

Take a few rod guides and tip-tops along with a spool of thread and some melt-type glue. Make sure that the tip-tops are slightly larger than the ones on your rod tip. That way, if the tip breaks off, the oversized tips will still fit. If the tip-top is too large, you can wrap the thread firmly around the rod tip to fill the space, and then add your melt-glue to secure it firmly.

I always carry a large Ziploc bag with a number of similar small bags inside. I use these for all sorts of things. They are perfect to carry spare napkins that can be kept dry to wipe your glasses. Your wallet and your paper money can be kept dry inside one of these bags. In the large Ziploc bag, I also carry an assortment of rubber bands—something you will always find use for.

In my pocketbook are always two or three Band-Aids. Every fly caster has at some time or another cut a groove into their stripping finger with the line. The fishing can get miserable without a Band-Aid. I've used a Band-Aid for other purposes, too. For example, a friend had a fly rod with ferrules that wouldn't stay attached. We pushed them as tightly as we could, then I wound a Band-Aid around the joint. It worked for the rest of the day until we could get home and have the rod repaired.

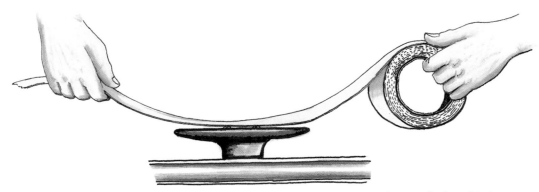

Cleats can grab your line and cause tangles. Bring masking tape to cover cleats and other objects on boats.

Masking tape is something else you should carry if you are fishing from boats. Cleats, ropes, boat pole holders, nails, and other objects will grab a fly line—especially during a critical cast. Have a roll of 2-inch masking tape to eliminate the problems. Even the guy owning a fancy yacht won't object to a little masking tape over an annoying cleat.

When sight fishing the flats for bonefish, tarpon, or permit, check the line on the deck regularly. This is a constant chore. I cannot tell you how line creeps underfoot. I sometimes swear I haven't moved my feet, but somehow the line gets under my foot and makes a cast impossible. You will encounter even more troubles if there

Always be on the lookout for line that is hung up on the boat or underfoot. You'll catch more fish and avoid causing damage to costly line.

Keeping spare line in buckets like these will help you cast more effectively and with fewer tangles.

is a breeze. The wind constantly shifts the loose line around. It tangles on itself, around cleats, along pieces of gear in the boat, and even on your own shoestrings. First of all, don't strip any more line off than you need to cast with. Additional line only means more opportunities for tangles. To avoid this trouble, plan where you will drop all of your loose line. I clear the area where the line will reside. I also try not to drop line on the same deck that I am standing on. I prefer to stand on what is called the casting deck (I like to think of it as the observation deck). I then make a cast and strip the line back, so that all loose line falls on the lower deck behind the casting deck. This helps me avoid standing on the line. Another advantage to depositing the line on the lower deck is that when the wind is blowing hard, the line stays on the lower deck because the boat sides create a windbreak.

Travel Lists

To arrive at a long-sought fishing destination only to find that you have forgotten a crucial item can ruin a great vacation. I rarely get caught without my essentials anymore. I have developed an all-encompassing list that serves me whether I'm going into the tropics or fishing on a cold fall day in New England. Add or delete items from the list below as appropriate for your trip and circumstances. If you develop a good list and check off everything each time, your future trips will be more pleasant and rewarding.

You can also stand on the casting deck and deposit the line on the lower deck.

Lefty's Trip List

Personal Items

Passport
Copies of passport pages
Visa (if needed)
Tickets
Letters and phone contacts
Reading materials
Notebooks—recorders—pens
Business cards
Thirty $1 bills
Extra money
Credit cards—checkbook
Shaving kit and extra blades
Sunscreen
Lipshield
Fishing license
Sunglasses—spares
Spare reading glasses
Maps or charts
Wrist watch spare
Sewing kit
Pocketknife
Spare keys
Toothpicks
Ziploc bags, napkins, and rubber bands

Fishing and Camera Gear

Rods
Reels
Lines and extra lines
Flies and lures
Hip boots and shoulder harness for
    hip boats
Nail clippers
Pliers and hemostats
Wading vest
Band-Aids
Krazy glue
Cigarette lighter
Cortaid and Stingeeze
Any medicines
Camera and extra bodies
Film
Lenses
Protective camera case or bag
Extra camera batteries
Shooting list
Lens cleaning liquid
Tripod

If you're traveling out of the country, keep a photocopy of your passport.

Clothing

Dress suit—shirts and pants
Light summer shirts and warm shirts
Dress socks and heavy socks
Light summer pants and warm pants
Light underwear and warm underwear
Spare belt
Sun gloves
Rain gear—two sets
Boat bag
Sneakers (two pairs)
Down vest
Fleece jacket
Hat and spare hat

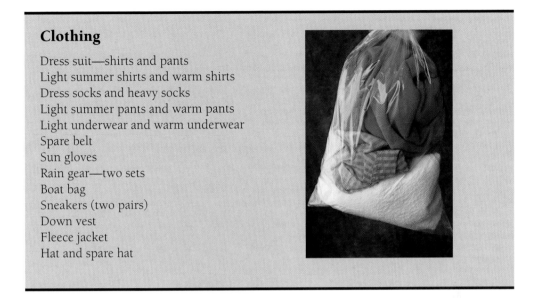

Fly-Fishing Myths

Fly fishing is the most traditional of all the angling sports, but tradition some-times results in the stagnation of ideas. There are techniques that have been sug-gested over the years about fly fishing that, in my opinion, should be regarded as myths. These myths in many cases prevent people from doing things better or having more fun or success with fly fishing. The following are some examples of ideas that the modern fly angler, regardless of how traditional he or she may be, should not hold.

If you cast with one hand, you should reel with the other. For example, if you cast with your right hand, you should reel with your left hand on the theory that if you hold the rod with the casting hand, you don't have to change hands to reel in line when a fish is hooked. And because your rod hand is stronger, you can pump the rod and fight the fish better with your stronger hand.

All of that is fine if you fish for trout in freshwater streams, which is where I think this myth developed. When almost any trout is hooked, it will run such a short distance that the amount of line that has to be recovered after each escape attempt is minimal. In this situation, it makes little difference whether you reel with either hand.

But there is a drastic difference when you set the hook in a saltwater fish that runs fast and takes out a lot of line. Bonefish, tarpon, and almost all larger offshore gamefish can and will quickly pull more than a hundred yards of line off the reel, re-peatedly, during the battle. With such long runs, the angler has plenty of time to switch hands. Either hand is strong enough to pump the rod. That takes little real strength. Your problem is not whether you can pump on the fly rod, but whether you are able to crank all that line back on the reel spool quickly enough to keep the line taut throughout the fight.

Many right-handed anglers claim that they wind a spinning reel with the left hand and have no trouble. But that reasoning doesn't apply when winding a fly reel. It's easy to turn a spinning reel handle because you are moving through a rather wide circle and the spool revolves about five times for every turn of the handle. A fly reel requires that you wind in very tight turns. Reeling in with such small circles is difficult to do with the "off" hand, especially when a lot of fly line has to be recovered quickly.

Use the lightest tackle possible. Many people feel that they are better sportsmen if they catch their saltwater fish on delicate 2-, 4-, or 6-pound-test tippets. Despite my great respect for the International Game Fish Association, I feel they have done the fish a great disservice by encouraging anglers to catch world records on very fragile tippets. Lactic acid builds up in the muscles of a fighting fish. Too much will kill them. By using those fragile tippets, you stand a good chance of prolonging a fish fight and killing the fish you so proudly release. It's my belief that you should always use a tippet strong enough for you to catch the fish, but weak enough to give the fish an even chance to escape. That is sportsmanship—not catching a big fish on a fragile line that may endanger its life.

Using the right rod for the fishing conditions is also the mark of an experienced angler. Using exceptionally light fly rods to subdue fish is not, in my view, good sense. To say that you caught a bonefish, snook, or redfish on a 4-weight rod, instead of a 7, 8, or 9, doesn't mean you are a better fisherman. I think it indicates a lack of concern for the fish—or an indication that an ego has to be stroked.

Anyone who has used spinning or plug tackle knows that if the rod is designed for ⅜- to ¾-ounce lure, you shouldn't try throwing a ³⁄₁₆-ounce bonefish jig or a 2-ounce chugger with this rod. It's possible to do it, but the rod will never function properly, and the angler won't be able to cast well. The same thing applies to fly fishing. When the manufacturer makes an 8-weight rod to match an 8-weight line, it was designed to throw flies of a specific weight or air resistance. For example, you wouldn't throw a big Popping Bug well with a 7-weight rod.

If you are inclined to use light fly rods (3 through 6) that are designed for freshwater fishing, consider what flies you will have to throw. A number of very large fish have been caught on tiny hooks, size 6 or smaller. But these small hooks grip so little of a fish's mouth that there is a good chance that the hook will pull free during the struggle. In short, you need to toss flies tied on hooks large enough to do the job. That means you should use fly rods that are well matched to the flies.

Lighter rods *can* be used for bonefish on days when the water is slick and the fish are spooky. However, I think a size 6 line is about as light as you should use. Of course, you could catch one on a 4- or 5-weight, because bonefish don't require a lot of butt pressure to bring them in. But if you want to throw a weighted crab, a Crazy Charlie, or one of the Clousers, I think a rod lighter than size 6 won't work well.

Lighter rods and lines develop less casting speed than rods a little heavier. This means that it is more difficult to make many casts with a rod that is lighter than more conventional rods. If the wind gets up, the light rod is going to make it more difficult to reach the fish. If you need to drive the fly back under the mangroves into a tight hole, a lighter line will make it far tougher to do.

There are a few situations in which lighter rods can be used, although one a

Flip Pallot with a baby tarpon.

few sizes larger would be better: for redfish, baby tarpon (I mean *real* baby tarpon), or bonefish when the wind is calm, the water is slick, and the fish are spooky.

Leaders should have a stiff butt and a limper forward section. When you make a forward cast and stop the rod in the direction of the cast, the fly line comes from straight behind you and unrolls toward the target. When the line has finally unrolled, the leader must do the same before everything is fully extended.

If the line is unrolling and it arrives at the stiff leader butt, that stiffer monofilament resists unrolling and wants to stand up and not turn over well. A heavy and limp butt section will unroll much better. Proof of this is the braided butt leader, which is super limp. Freshwater anglers who would be considered poor casters and who have difficulty in turning over a conventional monofilament leader have no trouble unrolling a braided butt leader because the braided leader is so limp. Of course, neither extra-limp nor very stiff monofilament is ideal for butt sections of leaders. The best monofilament for tapered saltwater leaders would be any premium spinning line.

You can't catch fish effectively at long distances. This is another myth promoted by anglers who are unable to cast a long line. I can't tell you how many times I have caught a fish by casting the full line—and sometimes the backing. If the hook is sharp and the line taut during the retrieve, long-line hookups are very effective, with the exception of hard-mouthed tarpon.

Fishing is always best early and late in the day. Again, this is not true. When light levels are low, early and late in the day, the fishing is *usually* better. But other factors can alter the situation. The best fishing can occur in the middle of overcast or rainy days, when the light levels are low. Fish do not have eyelids, and very bright days often mean that the fish will go deep and hide, waiting until light levels drop.

When fishing with Popping Bugs, allow the bug to sit motionless for long periods during the retrieve. A Popping Bug should be constantly moving almost all of the time when fishing in salt water. Creatures trapped on the surface seem to realize that they are vulnerable and that predator fish below will quickly eat them. A Popping Bug that is constantly moving creates the illusion that the bug is trying to reach safety as fast as possible. Indeed, in salt water, if you allow a Popping Bug to lie motionless on the water, most of the time the fish will move up to it, look at it, and then swim away.

Switch to a heavier line when casting in the wind. This is only partially true. If you are fishing distances up to 30 feet and have to cast into the wind, a line one size heavier will often allow you to load the rod better to deliver the fly. But if you are a fairly good caster and need to throw 50 feet or more, then you should do the opposite: switch to a line one size smaller.

For example, if you are using a 9-weight rod and switch to a 7-weight line, this will load the rod properly and you can throw tight loops longer distances. If you switch to a heavier-than-normal line, the rod flexes deeply and forces you to throw wider loops, which won't go very far in the wind.

Conservation

Finally, I would like to emphasize that we must take care of our fishing resources. Don't wait for someone else to save your fishing. Get involved in organizations that are fighting to save fish. It is surprising what citizens can do once they get involved. I think the Coastal Conservation Association has been responsible for much of the improvement in inshore fishing in this country the past few years—and it's made up of fly fishermen like you and me.

We should release most of our fish, too. No one burns their golf balls at the end of the day. We can catch a fish again only if we play it quickly and release it. I am totally against anglers who fish with 2- and 4-pound-test leader tippets for saltwater species. These battles are long and drawn out and often exhaust the fish to the point that it dies after it is released. We should use tippets that give both the angler and the fish a chance of winning.

How you put the fish back is also important to its survival. Gaffing a fish doesn't improve its chances when turned free. One of the finest tools for handling a fish you intend to release is the Boga Grip, a tool that doesn't hurt the fish, but allows you to hold it securely until it is released. Throwing fish back is not a good idea. Gently place them in the water. If possible, turn them back in shallow water. If the fish is still in trouble, it can be retrieved and resuscitated. Make sure any fish can swim well before letting it go.

Anglers who have always brought their fish home may change their attitude by your example. If we are going to continue to enjoy recreational fishing as we know it today, we all must take part in protecting and enhancing the fish that give us such great sport.

INDEX